Cheesecakes Made Easy

How to Make Knockout Cheesecakes without Knocking Yourself Out

Marcy Mallory

JPS Publishing Company
Grand Prairie, Texas

JPS Publishing Company
P.O. Box 540272
Grand Prairie, Texas 75054-0272

Publisher's Cataloging-in-Publication
(Provided by Quality Books, Inc.)

Mallory, Marcy.
    Cheesecakes made easy : how to make knockout cheesecakes without knocking yourself out / Marcy Mallory. -- 1st ed.
    p. cm.
    LCCN: 2001117730
    ISBN: 0-9664924-0-4

    1. Cheesecake (Cookery)   I. Title.

TX773.M35 2001   641.8'653
                                  QBI01-200879

CONTENTS

SECTION V: Fillings

Liqueurs

SECTION VI: Toppings

SECTION VII: Miscellaneous Information

REFLECTIONS

Rolling out dough for a gingerbread house last Christmas, I found myself reflecting on baking and life. As a child, I lined up mudpies to dry on boards in the sun—somewhere I'd seen a bakery! No, I didn't eat them or force them on my siblings.

The most consistent childhood highlight was going to my grandparents' house in Lubbock, Texas (the back seat was shared with Melinda, Marilyn, Phil and a German Shepherd named Hans). Memories include helping Grandmother fix meals, Granddaddy saying "She was the prettiest girl and the best cook." Their home was a place where I always felt loved, know what I mean? Visiting them as an adult, Grandmother always sent me home with a care package. She'd rummage through packages in the quilt-covered freezer in the garage. Often it was her fruitcake, the only one I liked. "I saved a little just for you." She probably said that to everyone, but it made me feel Really Special.

Suddenly, lulled into a meditative state by the sound and motion of the rolling pin, it dawned on me. Like Grandmother, I send out bits and bites of light and love with my cheesecakes and cookies. It's how I say "have a nice day" or "I'm glad we're friends" or "I love you."

Yes, I know many of you wish I cooked with fewer calories. Hey, love is rich! It never hurts my feelings to have my cheesecakes shared. So, bake with your hands and your heart, take a bite or two, savor the richness and pass it all on!

DEDICATION AND THANKS

This book is dedicated to myself for finally getting something done and crossed off my "someday I'm going to" list!

To those who are mirrors and teachers in my life: thanks for your reflections of truth, beauty, gentleness, kindness, compassion, friendship and love. I can only hope my reflections serve you and others half so well. For the always-increasing awareness that each moment is to be cherished I am forever grateful.

To all my friends, old and new: what would I do without you? Especially Carol, Lisa, Cindy and Carolyn, who always listen to my latest "life plans," knowing I'll not do 98.99% of them. Giant hugs. A special hello to everyone in Rochester, New York: your enthusiasm for taste-testing has not been matched. Don, thanks for the long phone consults on printing and marketing.

To all of my massage clients, especially Cynthia, Lynne, Linda, Robyn, and all the gang at Alpha Mortgage: thanks for your support and for taste-testing at the risk of adding body fat that you don't want me to see. You're all great. Thank you.

To Jerry Manion, for the custom kitchens "restored" in the 1895 Victorian and 1929 post-Victorian houses in Rochester years ago. They were great kitchens in which to pursue the art of making perfect cheesecakes. Thank you.

SECTION I
How To Use This Book

Beat cream cheese
Add sugar
Add flour
Add eggs
Add cream, half-and-half, vanilla
Pour into prepared pans
Bake, refrigerate, serve

Not long ago I made sixty plain cheesecakes to deliver all at once. Believe it or not, every single batch elicited a "mmm, it smells so good" when the aroma began to fill the kitchen and pervade the house. Even at 2:30 in the morning. Every time I opened the oven door to view a finished batch, I was excited when they turned out "right." More about that later.

The goal of this book is to demonstrate how easy it is to make cheesecake. In your own kitchen, with your own appliances and utensils, nothing fancier than a springform pan. It's fun and the results are amazingly consistent. Forget everything you've heard about how hard it is. The key is to master one basic recipe. The best approach is to skim through the book first. If you are a new baker or fearful of cheesecake baking, study the detailed sections. Then, pick your recipes and get going.

Section Two is an outline of the entire process. Section Three discusses the basic aspects. Handy hints, based on years of experience, are included here. Sections Four and Five give the basic crust and filling recipes in detail. The remaining recipes are grouped into crusts, fillings and fillings with liqueurs. Toppings are in Section Six and Section Seven is an odd collection of possibly useful information.

Beginning cooks, I hope you find this book helpful and encouraging. Experienced bakers, maybe you'll pick up a hint here or there, or be reminded of something you have forgotten you know. For those who love to eat, but not to bake—give this cookbook to someone who does cook, and invite yourself over!

The yield for each recipe is three 6-inch, or two 7-inch or one 8-, 9- or 10-inch cheesecake(s). Most of the time I bake 6-inch cheesecakes, usually two batches, or six at a time, in a thirty-inch oven. After I finished making the sixty cheesecakes, six at a time, I cooked twelve at once—that's six on each rack. It worked, but that might be pushing it a little at first. It's as easy to make and bake three or six at a time as it is one. If the filling is divided equally in the three pans, each cheesecake will weigh between one-and-a-half to two pounds, depending on the recipe. Baking three or six, you have plenty to serve, to give away,to take to work or to freeze. You can bake two flavors at the same time and offer guests a choice. Hey! Just like a fancy restaurant.

I read somewhere years ago, in a dark-and-sad novel about the regrettable but relentless decay of the South and genteel living, that one should always offer a man an alternative. I'd better quit here, and segue into the next paragraph with a straight face.

The 6-inch size is really easy to work with. It is easy to bake without cracking, easy to get out of the pan, easy to transport. These cheesecakes are not very sweet, but they are rich. Personally, I think it's more satisfying to savor a small amount of the real thing, rather than give up quality for less taste and more chemicals. But, that's just me. I serve reasonable portions and offers seconds. Offering alternatives and seconds—wow, I'm pretty cool! <u>The 6-inch cheesecake serves six to eight</u>, you aren't stuck with a lot to eat before it goes bad, and maybe there is a smidge less guilt with smaller portions.

One neat thing to enjoy is the change in texture and taste over a few days. They keep in a refrigerator for several weeks if well-wrapped, smooth out and get denser and heavier. They all need to sit at least twenty-four hours, in my opinion. My preference is the four-to-seven day range, or a month in the freezer. The heavier the better.

THE REAL KEY TO MAKING CHEESECAKE is to <u>bake only when you have time</u>, a leisurely two hours or so. Rushing doesn't work. You turn the mixer up too high, or don't beat long enough. Your right brain creativity is overpowered by your left brain trying to

keep on schedule. Working with a cold, or stuffy
sinuses, or on medications, seems not very effective
either. Ingredients get left out, eggshells fall where
they shouldn't, crusts gets burned, timers don't get
set, ovens don't get turned down, or get turned to
broil. Just to mention a few hypothetical possibilities.

Understanding the flexibility of these recipes is
also extremely helpful. It lessens the fear. It also
helps when you're ready to create your own specialties.
These proportions yield a medium to heavy, smooth,
creamy cheesecake that mellows into a heavier, denser
texture. You can make them without the heavy cream
and half-and-half, or with less amounts of either. Or
use all cream or all half-and-half. Less liquid makes a
heavier cheesecake. They work with less than three
pounds of cream cheese if someone has been nibbling
on it before you use it. Three eggs, or five, if you're
short one or need to use the last one, whatever size
you've got. If you have a sweeter tooth than I do, add
a little more sugar. Eggs, flour and cornstarch make
the cheesecake drier and "cakier." I don't like working
with cornstarch, so I use flour and eggs for firmness
control.

Stay in the range of about three pounds of
cream cheese and two cups liquid (total for cream,
half-and-half and/or liqueur). Ingredients like jam and
peanut butter work in the cup to cup-and-a-half range.
Sometimes I use one-and-a-half cups just to use a
whole jar, rather than have leftover bottles of dibs

and dabs. Chocolate works in the four-to-twelve ounce range. Start with eight ounces the first time and go from there as you experiment. Crust proportions are less flexible, but start with five tablespoons of butter and two tablespoons of sugar for each cup-and-a-half of cracker crumbs or nuts. Cookies need less butter and sugar than crackers.

When you compare these recipes with those in other books, you'll notice a wide range in proportions, as well as in cooking times. Over the years I've put together what works best for me. Do the same, and you'll be known as the one and only Ms./Miss/Mrs./Mr. Cheesecake in no time at all.

More ingredients = more filling
More liquids = more moist, creamy, softer
Less liquids = heavier, denser, less filling
More eggs, flour, cornstarch = heavier, denser

SECTION II
Brief Outline of All Steps

Crust

1. Place aluminum foil around outside of pans
2. Crush or grind crust ingredients
3. Cut butter, measure sugar, get vanilla out
4. Brown crumbs, add other ingredients
5. Divide crumbs into pans and pat down
6. Cook in pre-heated oven
7. Cool briefly and butter sides (if not done already)

Filling

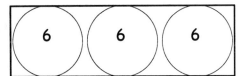

8. Beat cream cheese
9. Add sugar
10. Add flour
11. Add eggs
12. Add cream, half-and-half, vanilla
13. Add any other ingredients
14. Pour into prepared crusts
15. Bake, cool, refrigerate

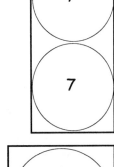

Serving/Storing

16. Take out, let sit, remove from pan
17. Garnish, if desired, and serve. Or,
18. Wrap and freeze

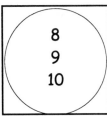

SECTION III
Handy Hints & Notes

Please note: I am not a professional food critic, chef, or baker, but why be picky.

Crust

Comments: To me, the crust is something to support the cheesecake, literally and figuratively. It should enhance the taste and add a hint of contrasting texture. Subtle support is the goal!

Utensils: *Cookware*: I have a 9-1/2 inch hard anodized *skillet* that I use for this purpose only. On low heat, the crumbs warm in the skillet without constant stirring. Cracker crumbs are bland and pick up subtle flavors. People with extremely sensitive taste buds will wonder about the faint aftertaste of bacon or garlic. I have several *wooden spoons* reserved just for stirring crumbs. Again, don't use a spoon that you leave in the vat of chili you simmer for hours for your annual Halloween parties, or Super Bowl Nine Million. Not that I ever know who's playing, unless the Dallas Cowboys are having a really good year.

There are several ways to crush crackers, cookies and nuts. My *blender/food processor* skills are really poor; for one thing, I always put too much whatever in at a time. Usually, I put a package of crackers or cookies in a plastic bag and roll them with a marble or wooden _rolling pin_. Handy note: using a bag, like the ones you bring veggies home in, with the printed side down can leave ink on your counter tops. An electric _mini-chopper_ works well for finely grinding crackers and most nuts also. I also use _grinding attachments on my KitchenAid® mixer_ and my _Saladmaster® Machine_ (thanks, Carol) to break up large quantities quickly, and then use the blender to grind more finely. A _hand chopper_ (I got mine at a Pampered Chef® party) is a fast way to chop nuts. Use what's quickest and easiest for you. Of course, you could buy packaged crumbs and nuts, right? Just don't tell me.

Personal note on rolling pins: Growing up, the only rolling pin in the kitchen had no handles. As an adult, with my own rolling pin, it took years to remember to use the handles. Even now, when I'm lost in automatic rolling mode so to speak, I find I'm using the pin and not the handles. However, the handles were put there for a purpose and do come in quite handy at times!

Springform pans or pans with removable bottoms: If you're going to be baking a lot you'll need several pans. These recipes yield crust and filling for three 6-inch pans, or two 7-inch, or one 8-,9- or 10-inch. Springform pans have two pieces: the bottom piece usually has a beveled rim and the collar (ring, rim, side) has a spring that releases at the first notch and opens up completely at the second notch. The bottom may be smooth or corrugated. They come in several sizes and materials, including nonstick surfaces, and some have handles on the collars (sides). Pans 8, 9 and 10 inches wide and 3 inches high are easy to find. Personally, I prefer aluminum, and really like the 6- and 7-inch pans best. Ten-inch and up require finesse. Glass slows down baking, and I just flat don't like how the nonstick surfaces or darkly-coated pans heat and brown. Plus, a real pet peeve is seeing scratch marks in the coating. It's all personal preference, of course, although I do recommend avoidance of corrugated bottoms.

Removable-bottom pans have a completely flat bottom piece to push up from the bottom. Be careful with both pieces, especially when they are brand new. Freshly milled edges are razor sharp.

Miscellaneous: Use <u>waxed paper</u> to line pans, and <u>aluminum foil</u> to wrap around the outside of the pans. Foil sheets are much quicker and easier to use. **Please recycle at least once, if you can.** Land is a limited resource, and there are better uses for this earth than landfills.

Ingredients: *Crackers*. Use the rectangular <u>buttery "club" crackers, not regular saltines</u>. Always use the lowest salt content crackers you can find, even if it means using "regular" instead of "low-fat." A major cracker company used to make low-salt club crackers, which were perfect, but I haven't seen them in years. Read the labels and compare sodium amounts. A few extra "regular" calories won't make any difference in your waistline or behind. The extra milligrams of salt will make a difference in taste.

Cookies: Use whatever you like, keeping in mind name-brands often have a stronger flavor that will carry through baking. Suggestions: ginger snaps, vanilla wafers, sandwich creams, shortbread, home-made gingerbread cookies, graham crackers.

Nuts: Be sure the nuts are not stale. Some nuts are harder than others. A thick crust of ground almonds and butter could be used for your dog's Frisbee® practice.

Cocoa powder: Use the best cocoa powder available—it makes a difference. Dutch-process is always a good choice. It's smoother and richer. Don't use cocoa mix—it's totally different.

Butter: **Use unsalted butter**. Find the word "unsalted" on the label, not just the word "sweet."

Vanilla: Real extract is better than "natural and artificial flavorings," but a small splash won't make much difference here. Mexican vanilla is stronger and distinct; use it only if you like the taste. Vanilla enhances sweetness without adding many calories. It's a nuance kind of thing, but use the best you can. I like the hiss and the aroma when it hits the skillet. Powdered white vanilla is also an option. It is strong, so use sparingly—which is a good thing, since it is expensive. A few granules in crust is wonderful.

Personal note on vanilla: My earliest memory of vanilla is when I was about ten. My dad (Otis B.) would fix pancakes for us on Saturdays every once in a while. One time he must have said he'd cook them if someone else made the batter. I don't remember if he or my mother showed me how, but I do remember him telling me to put a little vanilla in it, even if it wasn't in the recipe, to add a little flavor and sweetness. (Hi Daddy and Katie.)

Resources: I order spices, blocks of chocolate, nuts and vanilla from Tadco/Niblack in Rochester, New York. It's easier than finding and learning a new place and their stuff is great. Finding a place you like would be a good rainy day on-line project while cheesecake is in the oven. I've listed Tadco/Niblack information and a few websites for starters on page 125.

Preparation: Pan treatment is the biggest "personal preference" choice to make. Bill in Rockett uses waxed paper, foil and a water bath. It was a heated discussion. We're both Scorpios, and (maybe) both like being right. His wife, Cindy, was my friend way before she met him; she does a good job being patient with us. He's a good cook and baker. Their home is my private B&B retreat. Thanks!

<u>Waxed paper</u>: This works to line the inside of springform pans. <u>First option is</u>: Separate the pan. Put the bottom piece on the counter or table, and have the collar (sides, rim, ring) completely open. Put a piece of waxed paper over the bottom. Next, place the ring over the paper and the bottom. Press the paper down into the bottom as you snap the spring closed. That

keeps the paper from being stretched too tightly. Turn the pan over and trim the excess paper. Utility knives with replaceable "scalpel" blades work well. However, cutting with scissors works faster for me. Second option: tear off a piece of waxed paper bigger than the pan. Put the completely closed collar or the bottom on the waxed paper and with a knife or pencil score (mark around) the waxed paper around the pan. Move the pan, cut out the circle, and put it inside the pan. This works with both springform and removable-bottom pans.

Aluminum foil: You can do the same thing with foil and the first option. Be sure you press the foil down to conform to the bottom of the springform pan. With foil, you can gently tear the excess off, rather than use sharp instruments.

Some recipes suggest cardboard circles instead of the bottom piece, but it isn't worth the trouble. All of these options still leave you with the problem of leaking and dripping and smoking up the place. So,

WHAT I DO IS wrap a foil sheet around the outside of the pan and shape the foil up around the sides. I do not line the inside at all. Cake strips are available that can be wrapped around the sides of pans to help with heat distribution, etc. However, wrapping foil around the bottom and up the sides kills two birds with one stone, so to speak. Not that I'd ever kill a bird with anything, of course. The foil contains leaks and stabilizes the cooking environment.

A <u>combined technique using a foil sheet and a springform pan</u>: place the foil over the bottom (see first option under waxed paper). Carefully snap the collar on, and instead of turning the pan over and trimming the foil, just form the foil up the outside of the pan. Main drawback: foil tears at rim when snapped to close.

If you want to <u>butter the sides of the pan now, put the foiled pans in the icebox for a minute or two while you melt a little butter</u>. (I'm from Texas. I'm not old enough to have used real iceboxes, but the word was still used by parents and grandparents.) Brush the sides of the chilled pan with melted butter. Keep it light! The downside to buttering now is that crumbs will adhere to the sides when you form the crust, so you have to be neat. Another option, which is my choice, is mentioned in a page or two.

<u>Grind nuts and/or crush crackers</u>—see comments under utensils if you need help. If you're going for the ultimate, use a blender or food processor. If you just want close-to-perfect, use a rolling pin and roll as finely as possible. <u>Have butter measured</u>; just cut off what you need, using the guidelines on the wrapper. Don't waste time putting it into a cup and then the skillet. Be sure you don't put paper into the skillet. <u>Have sugar measured</u> and the bottle of <u>vanilla</u> (or powder) in reaching distance if you're going to add a splash or a dash.

Cooking: <u>Brown the crumbs in a heavy skillet over low temperature</u>. Watch carefully! Pull out any pieces of cracker or cookie that escaped being pulverized and crunch them with your fingers, or discard them. It seems to take forever for crumbs to warm and <u>start</u> to brown, but when browning starts it goes very quickly. If you have a sensitive nose and cook by smell, the instant you smell the crumbs pull the skillet off and stir. Turn heat down if necessary. IMPORTANT: what tastes barely, and I mean barely, burned will taste stronger in the finished product. It's cheaper to trash the crust and start over rather than trash the whole cheesecake at the last minute because suddenly you're embarrassed to bring it out. Serving to friends and family who take anything they can get is another story.

<u>Add the sugar or cocoa or nuts and stir continuously until well-mixed. Add the butter all at once and stir until absorbed and distributed evenly</u>. It should sizzle when it hits the skillet, but not splatter or melt immediately. Be sure all the crumbs are moist and there are no lumps of butter left. While the butter is melting, if the temperature is low enough and the skillet is heavy enough, you can leave it unstirred for a few seconds, but watch carefully. <u>Stir in vanilla quickly</u>. It's instant aromatherapy.

Often the crumbs will look too dry to form a sturdy crust. Resist the temptation to add more butter, or add just a small amount (less than a tablespoon). Cooking the crust will help it adhere. Remember, butter is hard when it's cold. A thick crust with a lot of butter might require a chisel to get the cheesecake out of the pan. Worse, an aftertaste of butter might not be the last thing you want guests to remember about your cheesecake.

    <u>Pull the skillet off the heat. Pour into foiled cheesecake pans; eyeball amounts or use a measuring cup</u>. There will be about three-fourths cup of crumbs per pan. <u>Shake each pan to evenly distribute the crumbs</u>. Then, depending on temperature of crumbs and sensitivity of your finger tips or the backs of your fingers, <u>pat the crumbs down firmly and evenly over the bottom of the pan</u>. If necessary, use a paper towel to protect your fingers; you can also use it to blot butter if you used too much. Make sure the crumbs cover the entire bottom to the edge of the pan, so filling will not leak. I don't build crust up sides, but feel free to do so. Obviously, the finer the crumbs and the firmer you press, the more compact the crust.

    Thickness of crust is personal preference. Try the recipe as is the first time, and then adjust. If there's a little too much crust for your taste, the easiest thing to do is make the recipe as given and then pull a few crumbs out before you compact it. Otherwise, you have to mess with all the ingredients to stay in balance. You'll end up calculating cumbersome measurements like one-half of one-third.

Place the pans into a pre-heated 400° oven. Set timer immediately for 7 minutes. When timer goes off take pans out and let them cool a minute or two. Crust should look a little bit brown and solid. However, don't poke or shake pan to check; let it cool down. Even on dark crusts (chocolate, for example) there will be a color change. Practice and observation help.

When pans have cooled enough to handle, butter the sides lightly if you didn't do it earlier. This is the other butter-the-sides option. Take a firm stick of butter, unwrap one end, steady pan in one hand, hold butter in the other and go around inside of pan quickly. I hold the butter and spin the pan around it. Work quickly so you don't use too much. The downside to buttering now is that you'll get a heavier coating, and it is harder to get sides covered down to the crust without gauging it. Don't worry about getting all the way to the crust. Gentleness counts here—don't scratch your counters with foiled pans, don't gauge crust with butter, don't drop the stick of butter into pan and don't hit crust with your hand or fingers. And if you forget to butter the sides, don't worry about it. Sometimes they come out just as cleanly without butter. Set aside—crust is ready to go! It's ok to make the crusts a day or two ahead. Just put them (cooked or uncooked) where they won't get jiggled or knocked around, and cover the pans with foil or plastic wrap.

Cheesecake Filling

Comments: As stated earlier, these recipes yield three 6-inch, or two 7-inch or one 8-, 9- or 10-inch cheesecake(s). The 6-inch size is really easy to work with and easier to bake without cracks and bubbles. More ingredients mean more batter, so a recipe with a lot of extras may fill the 6-inch pans nearly to the top. "Plain" filling will not fill a 9- or 10-inch to the rim, but the peanut butter and jam recipe completely fills a 10-inch pan. A 10-inch pan full to the rim is a little tricky to get in the oven without spilling, harder to cook without cracking and can be a little difficult to get out of the pan safely, but it is possible. Lowering temperature and increasing baking time will cut down on "puff" factor, which is discussed in a few pages.

Since I don't believe in covering up cheesecake, one of my main goals is a "no-cracks" surface. You can fill the pans nearly to the top and be ok. (See last sentence of last paragraph.) However, if you have extra filling, you can throw it away (which is impossible for me to do) or bake it in another pan. You probably won't have another crust handy, so you could try a light baking spray, or butter a pan and coat with flour—be resourceful. Who knows what you'll come up with! If you're making several batches, just layer them. Results can be pretty cool.

Utensils: <u>Mixer</u>: I use my KitchenAid® mixer, with the regular paddle. (My next one will be the their new 6-quart stainless steel mixer—it's beautiful. No, I have no deals with them, just love their mixers!) It might be tough on your arms and the mixer to use a portable one, but I guess it could work. Really, though, you need to have a *free-standing electric mixer* with a 4-1/2 to 5-quart bowl. A bowl with a handle makes it easier to pour filling but certainly isn't required.   A *spatula* or two, and *basic measuring utensils* are it. Pretty simple. A 1.5 liter (quart +) <u>stainless steel milk warmer</u> (looks like a really big metal measuring cup) is great for melting chocolate and is large enough to add filling to when you are making swirl (marble) recipes.

Mixer speeds vary, of course. I work in the "stir to 3" range, with an occasional "4." Stir is for mixing ingredients, stirring in fruits and nuts, adding liquids. Four is to mix semi-heavy batters, cream sugar and shortening, and so on. The more air you beat into ("incorporate" as they say on cooking shows) the cheesecake filling, the higher the potential for cracks; more air may also make the filling a little less creamy. The main thing to get here is: <u>slow (low) speeds rule</u>!

Personal note on mixers, life & relationships: I love my KitchenAid® mixer. In fact, I wish I had two to run during holiday baking time. About a year ago I scratched it and was upset for a week. I bought it nearly twenty years ago, when the prices weren't nearly so reasonable and you were liable to be labeled too fancy for your own good for wanting one. My *grandmother had given me some money. She liked it when we used her gifts for something special, rather than for household bills. I had a coupon, and still I waited for several months for the store to put them on sale. It was so hard to wait, but a lesson in life that some things are worth waiting for. My patience is <u>seldom</u> that practiced, but you know, nearly every time I turn it on I think of my grandmother! Jerry, who could spend hundreds on one saw and then another, never understood why I needed this mixer. The concept that it was a tool for me never sunk in. However, he got off my back about it a little when people would walk in to the kitchen and say "Oh, you've got a KitchenAid®." I think he was somewhat chagrined—he worked so hard to remodel a nightmare into a custom kitchen for me, and one of the first comments from guests was about my mixer! But then, it happened! One year, at a Christmas open house for Pavilion Street, neighbors came in, and the <u>man</u> started talking about the KitchenAid® they'd had for years, how he loved it, the quality and durability. So, I guess even kitchen tools have to be "man-approved" sometimes. At least, in my house it seemed to help, way back then. To be fair, Jerry washed a lot of cheesecake pans in the basement sink while he was remodeling the kitchen, and I needed to cook and my back went out. Getting up and down narrow stairs in the 1895 Victorian house on Averill Avenue to wash dishes in a huge sink in an unheated basement was more than I could manage.*

Ingredients: *Cream cheese:* Go to your local warehouse-type superstore and buy three-pound blocks of cream cheese. In my opinion, some cream cheese is better for cheesecake than others. Kraft® is so identified with cream cheese that you need to be ready to defend yourself if you don't use it! Most places won't have anything else, so usually it's a moot point. You can buy six 8-ounce packages, but it's more expensive and a pain to unwrap all of them. The price of cream cheese starts going up at the beginning of any holiday baking season. It usually has a long expiration date so it's ok to buy ahead to save a little money. Actually, "aged" cream cheese makes better cheesecakes.

A note about efficient shopping: When I shop I like to keep amounts of ingredients "balanced" so I have enough of everything if I decide to bake in the middle of the night or early in the morning. It truly annoys me to have to go to the store for one missing ingredient. One 3-pound block of cream cheese will require one cup of heavy cream and one cup of liqueur or half-and-half. You'd need two 3-pound blocks of cream cheese and one pint each of heavy cream and half-and-half to make six 6-inch cheesecakes. I use Keebler Original Club® Crackers and/or Waverly® Crackers. There are three packages in a one-pound box. One box is enough for three 3-pound blocks of cream cheese, which equals three batches, or nine 6-inch cheesecakes. Got the idea? Unless you have a natural flare for this kind of tracking, think through the recipe and the quantity before you go shopping. You'll save both time and aggravation.

Eggs: Use large or extra large, brown or white.

Heavy whipping cream and half-and-half: Like cream cheese, heavy (whipping) cream usually has a fairly long expiration date and enhances a dense, creamy flavor and texture. Half-and-half, on the other hand, will sour or go bad. Most supermarkets have quarts of half-and-half and heavy cream in stock, especially around holiday baking times. A few superstores have both, but don't assume they all do; you'll end up making another trip. I have used <u>frozen heavy cream and half-and-half</u>. Take them out a day or two in advance to thaw in the refrigerator—it takes a while. The thawed liquids may look a little bumpy, but they bake out just fine. Shake well before using, or blend for a few seconds to smooth it out. Actually, sometimes I think using frozen gives a creamier texture and taste.

Sugar and flour: Unless otherwise stated, sugar is always granulated (white) sugar, and flour is always unbleached, all-purpose white flour.

Chocolate—all forms: QUALITY MAKES A DIFFERENCE! Bakers who use good chocolate will recognize that you have also. Everyone else will know that your stuff tastes better than other people's stuff, but won't know why. Using good chocolate will mark you as a great baker faster than anything else. It's worth the extra money, even if you have to order.

Nuts: As mentioned earlier, make sure they aren't stale. Nuts literally may be stored in warehouses for several years as long as temperatures are kept cool. If there is any question, throw them away. Better to go to the store, leave them out or make a different recipe. Also, remember that hard nuts like almonds will be tough to cut through.

Candy and candy bars: Chocolate-coated and hard candies may "bleed" colors, but won't be noticeable in some recipes, and may leave pretty effects. Chunks of brownie or firm candy bars, like Snickers® for Cute Frank (he's married to my sister, Marilyn, and Viola is his 95-year old mom) in Las Vegas, will hold shape better than softer ones. Whatever you add, remember you'll have to cut through it after baking. You may need to coat pieces of "whatever" with flour to combat settling to the bottom. Or, alternate layers of filling with whatever you're adding.

Other stuff: Let's see: what else is there? Pineapple, coconut, pumpkin, flavorings, oil extracts. Size of pieces is a main consideration: heavy things sink and big chunks may be tough to cut through neatly. For example, crushed pineapple cuts cleaner than chunk pineapple, but chunks are more fun to bite into. Flaked coconut is the longer, moister kind; shredded is shorter and drier, and may distribute better and cut easier. Moisture content is a serious consideration when using fresh or canned fruit. I use oil extracts whenever possible, rather than flavorings.

Vanilla: Vanilla makes a difference here. Use the best "real" vanilla you can. Mexican vanilla is stronger, so be sure you understand the difference in taste. It's a matter of personal preference. Generally, I use Madagascar vanilla.

Liqueurs: Alcohol bakes out; normally, I use inexpensive brands, unless I want to make a specific name-brand recipe. Most liqueur cheesecakes need to sit (wrapped well and refrigerated) for three days up to a week. You can vary the "kick" by using more or less liqueur, staying in the 1/2-to-1-cup range. I always start with one cup, and seldom use more. <u>Use the liqueur in place of the half-and-half. Fillings with liqueurs tend to crack during baking.</u>

Personal note on using alcohol: **I always let people know when cheesecakes and truffles contain alcohol.** *Some do not want children to taste it, even though they (adults) know alcohol bakes out; some choose not to eat anything with alcoholic content for personal reasons. I've never had anyone be upset that I mentioned it, and often get thanked for being thoughtful. If you're entertaining and aren't sure, just offer a non-alcoholic flavor also—it's no big deal. You are learning to make two kinds at once, right?*

Preparation: <u>It's best to have everything at room temperature, but cream cheese is imperative.</u> It's much easier to work with, and the filling will be smoother. Remove the cream cheese from the box and use a sharp knife to make a cut down the length of the block, pull the plastic back and cut the block into chunks. Be sure the plastic coating does not get into the mixer. If you really want to zip through, let the cream cheese come to room temperature in the mixing bowl and have other ingredients measured. Break each egg into a small bowl and put all of them into a little bit larger one, so all four end up in one bowl. Eggs are seldom bad, like they used to be, but there is always eggshell-in-the-filling potential. You can still add them one at a time because each egg stays as its own individual little self as long as it isn't stirred or beaten. It's kind of neat, actually. Eggs, cream and half-and-half don't need as much time as cream cheese does to come to room temperature. I can't give an exact time for cream cheese, because refrigerators and room temperatures are different. I'd plan on one-and-a-half to two hours the first time, and see how it goes from there. Allowing it to warm in the carton takes longer than cutting it into pieces and putting into a bowl. Have the crust ready to bake, or already baked, or make it while you work on the filling.

<u>Beat the cream cheese, add and beat in sugar, flour, eggs one at a time, heavy cream, half-and-half or liqueur, vanilla. Pour into prepared pans</u>. Easy enough.

Baking: *This is where the art of cheesecake baking comes in*. The majority of these recipes are baked at 400° for fifteen minutes and then at 325° for one hour. When you review and compare recipes in other books you will find ranges from 300° for ninety minutes, to 375° for one hour, to 450° for twenty minutes and then reduced to 250° for one hour and everything in between. Find what works best for you.

You have to know your oven and understand heat distribution and relative humidity. If you are looking for something to be obsessed about, buy an oven thermometer and check the heat in the center and at the edges. Seriously, it's a good idea to check the temperature and make an adjustment if your oven allows that, or make a note to adjust the temperature accordingly each time. My new oven heated to 425° when it was set at 400°. Oven temperature is critical. If you have three 6-inch cheesecakes on one rack, the center one may be less brown because heat coming up the edges is blocked off. If you have six on one rack, the outside edges of the outside cheesecakes may be browner. Or not. If you bake twelve at a time the top rack will be browner and puffier. If you use both racks, remember the cheesecakes need "puff" room. Know your oven.

The fifteen minutes of higher temperature set the cheesecake. "Puffing," or rising/raising up/ expanding usually starts in the 35-to-50 minute range at 325°. If you want little or no browning and minimal puffing, then use lower temperatures and longer baking times, like seventy-five or ninety minutes at 300°. You just have to experiment.

A hint I've seen occasionally, but not tried, is to cover the cheesecake with foil if the top is browning too quickly. Most of the time, I want a little browning. If filling or butter drips onto the bottom of the oven and burns, the smoke turns the cheesecake a beautiful warm, golden color. Don't try it on purpose. It's a pain to drag a chair and broom over to the smoke detector.

As stated, I am not a professional food critic. Nor am I a rocket scientist. However, it is my opinion that humidity is the trickiest factor. Some recipes direct you to cook the cheesecake in a water bath. An easier way to get similar results is to put a pan of water on the bottom of the oven, or the bottom rack, with cheesecakes on the top rack. However, this gets to be tedious in a hurry. Not to mention downright annoying when you spill water all over the kitchen floor or the oven or into the cheesecakes. As cheesecakes cook they release steam. A hot, dry oven is more of a contrast than a cooler, more moist one. Think geyser here. Big build-up may mean big release may mean big cracks. For me, it's just easier to a:) beat slowly, b) reduce "peek" time and c) use lower temperatures with longer baking times.

ACCEPT THE FACT
THAT SOME DAYS CHEESECAKES WILL CRACK.
AND GET OVER IT.

Personal note on getting over it: Of course, I am not over it yet when I'm in a really picky, critical mood or selling them to someone new. No matter how many times I take cheesecakes somewhere and people assume they are from a bakery, or don't believe me when they found out I made them, I still want every single cheeseake to look perfect. By my standards. On my best "I am enough" new-age kind of days, I just hand them over with a smile. On not so good days, it is really hard not to explain the giant, glaring defects, which are highlighted by flashing neon signs. Fortunately, I've made vast improvement with this challenge, but that's not to say I don't backslide on occasion. (I'm shielding myself for friendly attacks from friends.)

Anyway, back to the "art side" of cheesecake. Humidity seems to stabilize the heat, tempers it somehow. On a dry day, the cheesecakes seem to cook faster and dryer, so they puff more. Yes, it's true, if the house is closed up and the thermostat is on 75°, it shouldn't matter if it's a winter 75° or a summer 75°. But most of us don't live in humidity-controlled houses. Heating our houses in winter really pulls moisture out of the air. Conversely, it may be less humid and sticky inside than outside, but some days you still stick to the floor and the furniture, at least in my part of Texas. When the environment is more stable, the oven heats more evenly and kicks on and off less often. That means fewer blasts of heat. The cheesecakes need consistent temperatures, not blasts of heat, or cold drafts. That's why you aren't supposed to open the oven at all. Oh, while I'm thinking about it, these cheesecakes tolerate slamming doors, kids running in and out, etc. Actually, they probably tolerate such things better than I do. So, don't worry about "don't-slam-the-door-I-have-a-cheesecake-in-the-oven" moments.

If you are baking in Arlington, Texas in winter and a blue norther blows in and drops the temperature 25° in thirty minutes, and the kitchen gets cooler, then the oven kicks on more. If you're baking in Rochester, New York in winter and people come in and out of the kitchen door, letting snowy blasts of 5° air in, the oven has to blast more. If you're cooking in the summer when it's 98° outside and 98% relative humidity (Arlington all summer, and Rochester on occasion), you may end up with really great cheesecakes. Like anyone but you would care on a day like that! Of course, at 98° and 98% RH, the house door doesn't open much because no one has energy to move that often or that quickly. So, on hot, humid days you can open the oven door with little effect on the cheesecakes. On cold, dry days, just look through the little window in the oven door. If you don't have a little window I guess you're up the creek. Most days I peek, even with a window. I can't help myself.

Toppings

In general, I don't believe in toppings for cheesecake. <u>Maybe</u> some fresh fruit or a light glaze of preserves or chocolate. However, a few recipes are included here. It's a good way to hide cracks. My main objection is that toppings often obscure the dynamic flavors I've worked so hard to achieve. In my opinion, pouring a can of pie filling over good cheesecake should be punishable by hanging. Yes, I'm old enough to remember cheesecake made with condensed milk and cherry pie filling on the top. Actually, I loved it way back then. Now, it's way too sweet. I might as well have pecan pie, which I love. **Have confidence and pride in your cheesecake creation; by itself, it is enough.**

Presentation

Presentation or "plate it up" means make it look nice! Decide whether to present it uncut, or pre-cut but whole, or as individual servings. You might display the cheesecake on the table or buffet "dressed" so people can see and admire it, and then quietly take it back to the kitchen to cut and serve. Or, cut at the table and serve. I think I most often serve individually, with no garnish. "I am enough" declares a piece of cheesecake able to stand alone. "I am enough" is one of my new-age life messages, if you haven't figured that out yet.

Acceptable garnishes include fresh fruit, fresh (edible) leaves, a drizzle of chocolate, a chocolate curl. Maybe a coffee bean or two, or thin slivers of crystallized ginger, or a nut, or a candied nut. Let your imagination go wild. Of course, the garnish should enhance the cheesecake visually. If garnish is meant to be eaten then it should enhance the taste also. For example, a few fresh raspberries and/or chocolate curls on a bittersweet chocolate raspberry, a row of chocolate chips or M&M's® down the middle of an individual piece of plain or chocolate or chocolate chip, a small dab of quality preserves on a plain, or raspberry on raspberry, strawberry on strawberry. A note about quality: homemade preserves are far superior. A side-note: seeded or seedless (berry) preserves is personal preference. I like the texture the seeds add, but not everyone agrees with me. (Hi, my friend Elizabeth in Rochester.)

The serving dish is an important consideration. Be creative. Practically, the cheesecake should be presented on a flat surface if it is to be cut and/or served from that dish. You'll need room to remove the pieces. Also, when using floss or a knife, you need room to pull straight out from the bottom of the cut—you cannot have such a small work area that you have to come back up and out through the cut. Never cut cheesecake on plastic wrap or foil. It creates a huge mess when you peel off strips and slivers; you'll be embarrassed when you see them left on the edge of a plate when you do dishes.

I like elegant presentations in the sense of simple and uncomplicated. Putting a chocolate marble cheesecake on a plate or tray with a busy pattern might be too much visual stimulus. The ubiquitous white paper doily may be used, but butter in the crust will leave oily spots which turn to neon oil slicks as soon as several pieces of cheesecake have been removed. Also, you might cut through the doily accidentally and have it drag or fold over and ruin the neat appearance you're going for.

To get the cheesecake out of the <u>springform pan</u>, take the pan out of the icebox, run a knife around the edges if needed, unspring the spring and let it stand for ten or fifteen minutes. Then carefully release the latch completely and lift collar up and off.

Pay attention and don't gauge your masterpiece; you may have to gently push the cheesecake up through the ring. Watch for sharp edges; blood isn't an acceptable topping under any circumstances. Gently insert the tip of a knife between the cheesecake and the bottom of the pan to release it. You may have to insert several times, at quarter turns, maybe. You'll feel or sense the release (I'm an energy worker). Have plastic wrap, cutting board or serving tray ready. For <u>removable bottom pans</u>, let them sit out for ten or fifteen minutes and then push the bottom up through the collar. If there is resistance, wait a few seconds and push again. It always surprises me how well it works. The only reason it wouldn't is if butter leaked from the crust and sealed it. In that case, just turn the pan over and loosen the stuck parts. Be really careful working with these. Sharp edges!

I have a long, long knife that cuts across a 10-inch cheesecake in one straight down motion. You can't "see-saw" cheesecake. Smooth, creamy, soft textures will look mangled on the cut edges; firmer, denser ones will be cleaner and more even, but still need careful cutting. Cheesecakes with nuts, candy bars, chunks of brownies or cookies, chips, etc., get trickier to cut neatly, especially with a knife.

To get a clean cut use dental floss. The next best option is a warm knife, but filling will still stick, so you'll need to rinse or wipe knife between cuts.

Handy hints on cutting: as stated, dental floss works best. Have the cheesecake on a flat surface (pedestal cake stand is perfect). Use enough dental floss to hold tautly and push straight down through entire cheesecake. Using thumb or finger, hold one end of floss down on surface and with other hand pull floss straight out from bottom of cheesecake. Try to keep the floss on the flat surface as you pull it; otherwise, you rough up the cut.

The same method is used with a knife. Make one clean, quick cut straight down, and pull the knife straight out from the bottom. Do not using a sawing motion or bring the knife back up through the cheesecake. Wipe the knife clean between cuts with a warm cloth. If you have a very firm cheesecake, you might get away with two cuts before you need to wipe the knife. If you have a knife with the middle of the blade cut out, try it. But again, cut straight down and out. **Don't saw.**

Now it's cut. For individual servings, gently slide tip of knife or spatula or fork under piece of cheesecake, put it on plate, garnish if desired, serve and get ready for the compliments! Good coffee always goes with great cheesecake. It's one of those "ahhh " moments in life. If you'd like, find a creative combo of flavored coffee and cheesecake. My favorite is a piece of "Just Plain Great" with a cup of dark Colombian coffee, shared with a friend.

Storage

Cheesecakes can be stored up to three months, especially in a non-automatic defrost freezer, with no real change in quality. By then, the crust may start to taste a little stale and the filling may be a little dry. I've kept them up to nearly a year and received great feedback, but don't recommend forming that habit. Quality goes down faster in self-defrosting freezers.

They last several weeks in the icebox (you know, Texas) if wrapped well. As with all cheeses, mold is a potential problem. I wrap everything in three layers of plastic wrap. The easiest thing to do is go to your local superstore and buy a big, extra-wide roll of plastic wrap (film). The extra width makes wrapping much easier. It's a huge package; write the date on the box and see how long it lasts. You'll hate the regular size you buy at the super market once you've used the "industrial" size!

For those of you who eat frozen cheesecake: I can't help you save yourself. My sister, Melinda, once told me she tried putting it in the freezer so she wouldn't be tempted, but in the middle of the night the cheesecake would call out to her. Then, she'd have to eat it frozen! Several other people have spontaneously volunteered that freezing doesn't slow down consumption much at all. Maybe you could cut the cheesecake into very small serving pieces and wrap them individually. At least you wouldn't have to wake up enough to unwrap a whole one, chisel a chunk off to eat, rewrap the rest, eat it and then go back to bed.

A note about serving cheesecake that has been frozen: thaw it in the refrigerator if there is time. It will cut easier and cleaner at room temperature, and won't crumble as much during consumption. My preference is room temperature cheesecake. It's easier and more fun to explore texture and taste.

Cleanup

Don't let the pans sit out and get dry. If a little crust or filling sticks, no biggie. It's a good way to taste-test. Usually I wash pans in hot soap and water by hand but I do throw them in the dishwasher occasionally. All my pans are aluminum, but if you have tin or steel, remember rust potential.

Finally, the recipes! Turn the page to begin your own cheesecake adventures.

The best handy-dandy cooking hint I ever received, bar-none, was from Aunt Polly (Hi, Uncle DC). I was fairly young and making peanut butter cookies. The cookbook said to dip the fork in water before making crisscrosses to flatten the cookies, but the dough stuck. I must have been sighing loudly or muttering to myself: I wanted ease and perfection even then. Unaware she was watching, I heard her say from across the room "If you'll dip the fork in flour first the dough won't stick." It was such an easy solution, unexpected but so well-timed; my anxiety level dropped immediately and I was happy again. It hadn't occurred to me to ask for help. Hmm, are there life lessons in here somewhere?

SECTION IV
Crusts

Plain Crust, Detailed Directions

<u>Yields enough for:</u>
three 6-inch OR two 7-inch OR one 8-, 9-, or 10-inch

1-1/2 cups fine buttery "club" (rectangular) cracker
    crumbs (1 package)
2 tablespoons granulated sugar
5 tablespoons unsalted butter
Splash vanilla

    Assemble pans; wrap foil sheets around bottom
and up sides. Butter sides now (p. 20), if preferred, or
wait until baked (p. 23). See Section III (p. 18) for
options on pan preparation.
    In heavy skillet, over LOW heat, warm crumbs
until you just begin to smell them, or until the crumbs
are fairly warm to the touch. If you wait until they
start getting light brown it may be too late. Stir
constantly unless you have a heavy pan and low enough
heat, and then still watch carefully.
    Sprinkle sugar over crumbs and stir in quickly.
Add butter and stir until melted. Add vanilla and stir in
quickly. Mixture should look moist but not sticky.
    Divide equally into cheesecake pans. Shake
gently to distribute crumbs. Let cool a minute and then

press down evenly with fingertips or backs of fingers. Use a paper towel for heat protection, if necessary. Make sure crumbs are pressed over entire bottom plate to avoid leaking. Bake in preheated 400° degree oven for 7 minutes. Take out of oven immediately. Crust will look just a little bit browner; it's a subtle change. Let cool a few minutes and then butter sides, if not done previously.

Keebler Original Club® Crackers

- 1 package = just under 12 ounces or 1-1/2 cups of very fine crumbs. Use blender or processor to get this fine; if you squeeze a handful of crumbs in your hand and then open your fingers, the crackers will retain knuckle prints. Makes best crust but it's a pain to do in my blender.
- 1 package = just over 12 ounces or 1-1/2 cups crumbs of fine crumbs using a rolling pin. Put crackers in plastic bag and roll until crushed.
- 1 package = about 12 ounces or 1-1/2 cups in something like mini-chopper and seems to be good compromise—fast to do and crumbs are small enough.
- There are 45 crackers in 1 package, and 3 packages in a one-pound box. One package of crackers is enough for one recipe, or three 6-inch crusts. Therefore, one box is enough for nine 6-inch crusts total.

Waverly® Crackers

- Waverly Crackers have 40 crackers in a package, and may measure a little less than 1-1/2 cups. Use the same amounts of butter, sugar and vanilla.

Chocolate Cookie

1-1/2 cups fine chocolate sandwich cookie crumbs
1 tablespoon sugar, if desired
1-1/2 tablespoons unsalted butter
1 teaspoon vanilla

Chocolate Cookie and Nuts

1/2 cup finely chopped nuts
1 cup fine chocolate sandwich cookie crumbs
1-1/2 tablespoons cocoa powder
1-1/2 teaspoons vanilla
3 tablespoons unsalted butter

<u>All recipes yield enough for</u>:
three 6-inch OR two 7-inch OR one 8-, 9-, or 10-inch

In heavy skillet, heat crumbs over LOW heat until you just begin to smell them or until warm to touch. Stir frequently. Add sugar and/or cocoa powder and/or nuts and stir in. Add butter and stir until melted and well-mixed. Stir in vanilla. Mixture should be moist but not clump together. Divide into prepared pans. Press firmly, making sure entire bottom plate is covered. Bake in preheated 400° oven for 7 minutes. Remove immediately. Cool for a minute or two and then butter sides, if not done previously.

Chocolate Graham Cracker

This is fast and easy. Thanks, Carolyn, for keeping after me about graham cracker crusts.

1-1/2 cups fine graham cracker crumbs (15 full-size, or 1-1/2 packages)
4 tablespoons unsalted butter
1 teaspoon vanilla
1-2 tablespoons sugar, if desired (I don't use)

This makes a lot of crust. If preferred, use 1 cup crumbs (1 package crackers) and 3 tablespoons butter—you might have to work a little to get all three pans covered with crust, but it's manageable.

Cocoa Powder

Intense chocolate taste.

1-1/2 cups fine buttery club cracker crumbs
3 tablespoons cocoa powder
3 tablespoons granulated sugar
5-1/2 tablespoons unsalted butter
1-1/2 teaspoons vanilla

It's subtle, but baked crust will look drier and more solid, or set, and color will be different. Resist temptation to add more butter until you've tried recipe a time or two.

Ginger Snap Crust

The saga! I have not been able to produce a ginger snap crust that doesn't get soggy. I'm talking about baked crusts. I have tried recipes from books, magazines, box tops, my head. No matter what the ratio of crumbs to butter, or temperature, or minutes cooked. The taste is excellent, especially with plain or pumpkin fillings. Maybe people don't know any better, because I always get lots of compliments. Maybe they are just being kind.

1-1/2 cups fine ginger snap cookie crumbs
1 tablespoon sugar, if desired
1/2 to 1 teaspoon ginger, if desired
1 tablespoon unsalted butter, if desired

Yield:
three 6-inch OR two 7-inch OR one 8-, 9-, or 10-inch

In heavy skillet, heat crumbs over LOW heat until you just begin to smell ginger. Stir frequently, even in a heavy skillet, because the crumbs will be sticky as soon as they start to warm up. Stir in sugar and/or ginger, if you are using them. Add butter and stir until melted and well-mixed. Mixture should look moist but not clump together. Divide into prepared pans, cool briefly. Press firmly, making sure entire bottom plate is covered. Bake in preheated 400° oven for 7 minutes. Cool a minute or two and butter sides, if not done earlier.

Notes: Adding ginger really enhances the flavor of the ginger snaps. If you use snaps that are really "gingery" you might want to try it without adding extra the first time. It may take a few times to get this one just perfect. The crust will get soggy, so plan to eat these fairly quickly. Placing the cheesecake on a paper towel and then in plastic wrap works in the icebox and in the freezer.

Because gingerbread cookie recipes usually call for shortening, I overcame my buttery snobbery and made crust with 1 teaspoon of shortening—gross! I tried just crumbs, lightly toasted, put in the pan and pre-baked as usual. Still got soggy, but not so quickly. Tried thin layers (too thin, and it leaks) and thick layers.

I will state that I seem to be the only one completely obsessed about this. Good luck, and feel free to contact me if you figure it out!

Using homemade gingerbread cookies is another option, but it's been so long that I don't remember the results clearly. I'll let you know in the next edition.

At this writing, I use 1-1/2 cups of crumbs with 1 teaspoon ginger added, lightly browned in heavy skillet, pressed into cheesecake pans and heated in 400°for seven minutes.

Hardly Any Crust at All Crust

1 cup fine buttery club cracker or cookie crumbs
1 teaspoon butter

Lightly brown cracker or cookie crumbs in nonstick skillet, add butter, stir until melted. Divide equally into three 6-inch cheesecake pans. Pat down, completely covering bottom plate. It will be thin. Cook at 400° for 7 minutes and remove immediately. Butter sides if desired, but if low calorie count is the purpose, then leave unbuttered.

Light Crust

1-1/2 cups fine diet bread crumbs*
1 stick butter
1 to 2 tablespoons sugar

Very lightly brown bread crumbs in non-stick skillet, add sugar and butter, stir until melted and blended. Divide into three 6-inch cheesecake pans. Pat down, completely covering bottom plate. Bake at 400° for 7 minutes and remove immediately. Butter sides if desired, but if lower calorie count is the purpose, leave unbuttered.

*Dry 8-12 slices of diet or low-calorie bread in oven, then grind or crush. Size of slice will determine how many slices you need.

Nut

1 cup fine buttery club cracker crumbs
1/2 cup finely ground nuts
2 tablespoons sugar
5 tablespoons butter

Brown cracker crumbs and nuts in heavy skillet until just warm to touch. Stir in sugar, add butter and stir until melted. Divide into three 6-inch pans and bake in preheated 400° oven for 7 minutes. Remove from oven immediately, cool briefly, and butter sides if not done earlier.

Notes: Pecans and brown sugar are a good combination. Vary amounts of nuts and cracker crumbs, if you'd like, but remember that some nuts are hard to cut through. I wouldn't go more than about three-fourths cup of nuts, especially with almonds.

SECTION V
Fillings

Just Plain Great, Detailed Directions

Have crust ready to bake before you start the filling. Or, work on them simultaneously, but it's easier to have the crust made ahead until you have sequences incorporated into your own baking style.

3 pounds cream cheese, room temperature
1 cup granulated sugar
1/3 cup all-purpose flour
4 large eggs, room temperature
1 cup heavy (whipping) cream, room temperature
1 cup half-and-half, room temperature
1 tablespoon vanilla

1. Beat cream cheese in large mixing bowl on low speed about 5 minutes, until smooth and shiny; scrape 2-3 times during mixing. "Scraping" means scrape the bowl and beater(s). NOTE: Bowl scraping needs to be done more often if mixer doesn't mix everything on the bottom.
2. Add sugar and beat on low for 2-3 minutes, scraping at least once. Texture looks smoother.
3. Shake flour over batter and beat at low speed until flour is mixed in; texture looks bumpy. Increase speed one notch and beat 3-4 minutes, scraping several times. Batter will get thicker and duller looking.

4. At low speed again, add eggs one at a time;
beat well after each. Scrape after 2nd and 4th eggs.
NOTE: Once eggs are added filling gets thinner, so
scrape gently to avoid adding air bubbles. After last
egg, scrape and then beat on medium-low for about
2 minutes.

5. With mixer back on low, add heavy cream and
half-and-half (together or separately) slowly and mix
for another 3-4 minutes. Add vanilla, beat 2 more
minutes. Lift beaters and let drip back into bowl.
NOTE: Do not scrape beaters at this point; large
chunks of cream cheese will stay that way.

6. Pour into 3 prepared 6-inch cheesecake pans.
Bake in preheated 400° oven for 15 minutes, then
reduce heat to 325° for 1 hour. Turn oven off and
leave cheesecakes in oven for 2-3 hours with door
closed, or until pans are comfortable to touch.

♥Refrigerate, Room, Release, Serve, Store♥

7. Take cheesecakes out of oven and admire
them for a moment. **REFRIGERATE for several hours
or until completely cooled. Overnight is best.** Run a
knife around the edge to loosen the cheesecake, if
necessary, before you put it in the icebox. You can tell.

8. **Take out, unsnap springform ring to first
notch and let stand for 10 or 15 minutes at ROOM
temperature.** Have plastic wrap or serving dish ready.

9. Run knife around edge if needed. Hopefully, it's pulled away from sides. For springform pan, **completely RELEASE clasp and lift collar (side) straight up and off, or push bottom up through rim.** Pans get a little bent out of shape over time, so pay attention not to gauge. <u>My definition of a perfect cheesecake is one that has no cracks, is nicely browned on top, and has pulled in from sides with a smooth, slightly browned, dry look around the edges</u>. Usually the bottom comes straight up or the rim lifts off easily. However, for some reason I occasionally have to put one hand under the cheesecake and push up through rim in order not to gauge the sides. **For regular pan (no clasp) with removable bottom**, push cheesecake from bottom up through sides. If it sticks, wait a second or two and try again. It works, really. Use consistent, steady pressure. If necessary, you can turn the cheesecake upside down on counter and then pull the rim off, or push bottom down toward counter slowly. Either way, watch for sharp edges! About now you'll begin to appreciate working with these sizes.

10. To separate the cheesecake from bottom, **put the edge of a knife between the crust and pan and gently pry.** With very little effort you should feel the entire cheesecake release. If not, pry another place or two. Inserting and prying at quarter turns is nearly always enough. Even a soft-textured cheesecake should be "handleable" at this point. Put cheesecake on serving tray, or on plastic wrap. If you used the same

foil sheet to line the inside bottom and wrap the outside, gently remove it, and you're done. If you used waxed paper, be sure it gets removed as well.

11. **Prepare for SERVING** (see Presentation, page 36) **or STORING** (page 40), as discussed in previous sections.

How to Tell When Cheesecake is Done

The cheesecake will look dry, set, and a little dull. It will be a slightly different color, depending on ingredients and moisture content. Experience helps tremendously. The center will still be a little soft and will kind of shimmy if you move the pan. Again, experience helps. It shouldn't wobble all over the place. It firms up sitting in the turned-off oven and continues to firm up when cooling in the refrigerator. A perfect cheesecake will be barely, but completely, shrunk from the sides of the pan. The absolute worst you'll have the next day is a really soft texture, which you present as an intentionally really moist and creamy-like-pudding cheesecake. Don't panic—it's not nearly as bad as fudge that won't set, or brownies that refuse to get done in the middle. Remember, cheesecake gets heavier and denser over time—in other words, it'll dry out.

Apple Walnut

10-20-89: sold this one at an apple mill near Rochester, NY for a while. Great for breakfast or brunch, especially in the fall.

3 pounds cream cheese, room temperature
1-1/4 cups granulated sugar
1/3 cup all-purpose flour
4 large eggs, room temperature
1 tablespoon vanilla
2/3 cup heavy cream, room temperature
1/3 cup half-and-half, room temperature
***

2-3 cups peeled, chopped apples (2-3 large apples; I
    use Granny Smith, but it's personal preference)
1 cup chopped walnuts
2-3 tablespoons brown sugar (dark is more flavorful,
    but personal preference again)
1 slightly heaping tablespoon all-purpose flour

     Beat cream cheese in large mixing bowl on low speed about 5 minutes, until smooth and shiny; scrape 2-3 times. Add sugar and beat on low for 2-3 minutes, scraping at least once. With mixer on low, shake flour over batter and beat in. Increase speed one notch and beat 3-4 minutes, scraping several times.

     At low speed again, add eggs one at a time; beat well after each. Scrape gently after 2nd and 4th eggs, then beat on medium-low for 2 minutes. With mixer back on low, add heavy cream and half-and-half slowly; mix for another 3-4 minutes. Add vanilla, beat 2 more minutes. Lift beaters and let drip back into bowl. Pour into 3 prepared 6-inch cheesecake pans.

<u>Combine apples, walnuts, brown sugar and flour in medium bowl</u>. Mix with large spoon or by hand; work quickly, but thoroughly coat apples. Put apple and walnut mixture* on top of cheesecakes. Bake in preheated 400° oven for 15 minutes, then reduce heat to 325° for 1 hour. Turn oven off and leave cheesecakes in for 2-3 hours, or until pans are comfortable to touch. ♥Refrigerate, Room, Release, Serve, Store♥

Notes: There is less filling in this recipe on purpose—to leave room for the apples and walnuts, and to have a heavier base to support the topping.

*I peel and cut the apples after I pour the filling into the pans, then add the walnuts, sugar and flour. Cut the apples into fairly large, but still bite-size pieces. Mix by hand until well-coated and then distribute. If you mix too early you'll have juice and soft apple chunks. If that happens, just shake the juice off before you put the mixture on. If desired, add a little cinnamon, cloves or nutmeg to the mixture.

Banana with Chocolate Glaze

For Janice and Patsy. This one is delicious with or without the chocolate glaze. Creamy and smooth. Plain crust works, but chocolate nut crust works better. The bananas add a golden hue.

3 pounds cream cheese, room temperature

1-1/4 cups granulated sugar

1/3 cup all-purpose flour

4 large eggs, room temperature

1 cup heavy cream, room temperature

1 cup half-and-half, room temperature

1-1/2 cups mashed bananas (about 4 small, fully ripe but not overripe)

1 tablespoon vanilla

Chocolate glaze (see Toppings on page 116, or use your favorite)

Beat cream cheese in large mixing bowl on low speed about 5 minutes, until smooth and shiny; scrape 2-3 times. Add sugar and beat on low for 2-3 minutes, scraping at least once. With mixer on low, shake flour over batter and beat in. Increase speed one notch and beat 3-4 minutes, scraping several times.

At low speed again, beat in eggs one at a time. Scrape after 2nd and 4th eggs, then beat on medium-low for 2 minutes. With mixer back on low, add heavy cream and half-and-half slowly; mix for another 3-4 minutes. Add mashed bananas and vanilla, mix well for several minutes. Lift beaters and let drip into bowl.

Pour into 3 prepared 6-inch cheesecake pans. Bake in preheated 400° oven for 15 minutes; then reduce heat to 300° for 75 minutes. Turn oven off and leave cheesecakes in for 2-3 hours, or until pans are comfortable to touch. ♥Refrigerate, Room, Release, Serve, Store♥

To serve with chocolate, allow cheesecake to come nearly to room temperature. Coat with your favorite chocolate glaze and chill or set, as needed.

Notes: This will need a knife run around pan sides before refrigerating. To get a smooth, dry look around the edges, bake for up to 90 minutes.

Presentation Fun: Serve individual pieces with warm chocolate glaze on top and drizzled down sides. Place sliced banana and maraschino cherry on top, and maybe a nut. A banana split cheesecake sort of deal!

Chocolate chip glaze (page 116): Melt 3 ounces (about 1/2 cup) semi-sweet chips and 1/4 cup heavy cream in a heavy, non-stick sauce pan on LOW heat. Stir occasionally until melted. Spread on cheesecake and refrigerate to set, or serve as warm drizzle. Thickens at room temperature, but warms up in microwave beautifully. Chocolate-glazed desserts are sticky to cover and transport in hot, humid weather. Make the glaze at home, put it in a microwave dish and warm it when you're where you're going. Or take ingredients and make glaze on-site.

Brownie Chunk

This is Just Plain Great with chunks of brownie thrown in. You can use a thin layer of brownie batter for crust; cook the crust completely first. You may find it tough to get the crust not to be gooey in the middle. For "double" brownie indulgence, add a cup of cocoa powder to the cheesecake filling.

3 pounds cream cheese, room temperature
1 cup granulated sugar
1/3 cup all-purpose flour
4 large eggs, room temperature
1 cup heavy cream, room temperature
1 cup half-and-half, room temperature
1 tablespoon vanilla
Geoff's Brownies (see below) or your favorite

Beat cream cheese in large mixing bowl on low speed about 5 minutes, until smooth and shiny; scrape 2-3 times. Add sugar and beat on low for 2-3 minutes, scraping at least once. With mixer on low, shake flour over batter and beat in. Increase speed one notch and beat 3-4 minutes, scraping several times.

At low speed again, add eggs one at a time, beating after each. Scrape gently after 2nd and 4th eggs, then beat on medium-low for 2 minutes. With mixer back on low, add heavy cream and half-and-half slowly; mix for another 3-4 minutes. Add vanilla, beat 2 more minutes. Lift beaters and let drip into bowl.

Add as many bite-size brownie chunks as you want to and fold in with rubber spatula. Pour into 3 prepared 6-inch cheesecake pans. Bake in preheated 400° oven for 15 minutes, then reduce heat to 325° for 1 hour. Turn oven off and leave cheesecakes in for 2-3 hours, or until pans are comfortable to touch. ♥Refrigerate, Room, Release, Serve, Store♥

Notes: These brownies are always welcomed. Try putting a layer of chocolate chips on the top before you bake them. I call these "Geoff's Brownies" for Geoffrey Schantz, who succumbed to heart disease at the age of 9 in 1986. His parents used bites for reward, enticement, encouragement; Geoff liked them and they were low in sodium. That was a year of losses for me; his was the toughest, even though he wasn't related. I can't imagine such pain, but offer compassion and love. In this world of tragedies and miracles, his as-yet-unborn sister required a heart transplant at the age of 10. I'm happy to report Ali is now 13 and doing well. Organ transplant can be a good thing.

Geoff's Brownies

1-1/2 cups butter	1-1/2 cups flour
3 cups sugar	1 cup cocoa powder
1 tablespoon vanilla	1/2 scant teaspoon baking powder
4 large eggs	1/4 scant teaspoon salt

Cream butter, sugar and vanilla thoroughly. Add eggs one at a time, mixing well. Stir dry ingredients together and beat into butter mixture for several minutes. Bake in greased and floured 15 x 10-inch pan at 350° for 45-50 minutes, or until brownies begin to pull in from sides of pan. Cool, cut and indulge!

Butter Cookies

This bonus recipe is great for holidays. It rolls out really thin, cooks to a beautiful color, tastes delicious and looks fantastic decorated. It's in this book because I had to put something on one page and it's requested often. Actually, it might make good crust. Can't remember if I've tried it or not, but feel free.

1 cup butter, room temperature
1 cup granulated sugar
3 large eggs
3-1/2 cups all-purpose flour
1 teaspoon baking powder
1/4 teaspoon salt
1 tablespoon vanilla

Measure flour, then put baking powder and salt on top of flour and cut through several times before adding to dough.

375°, 8-10 minutes, or until pale brown, and a slight nudge releases cookies from baking sheet.

Cream butter and sugar completely. Add eggs one at a time; beat well after each. Beat in vanilla. Slowly add flour, baking powder and salt. It's a heavy dough, but thorough mixing is crucial to avoid streaks. Put in waxed paper and then in plastic wrap or bag. Chill several hours. Let sit at room temperature for 15-20 minutes before you work with it. Roll on floured board to desired thickness, cut out, bake on ungreased sheet. Hint: take out of oven and nudge with spatula to Release. Cool completely before removing from sheet to avoid structural hairline fractures.

Carrot Cake

Based on a carrot cake recipe from Cindy McConologue in Rochester, New York. Most recipes for carrot cake have allspice, cinnamon and/or nutmeg. I like the flavor of the mace, and I loved her carrot cakes. This recipe is really rich, especially with the topping. (Yes, you are allowed to put a topping on this one.) Mace is expensive and sometimes a little hard to find in grocery stores.

3 pounds cream cheese, room temperature <u>PLUS</u>
<u>one 8-ounce </u>package for topping (or use 8 ounces
    from the 3 pounds—it still works, and gives a
    heavier cheesecake)
1-3/4 cups granulated sugar
1/3 cup all-purpose flour
4 large eggs, room temperature
2 cups small peeled carrots, finely grated
    (equals about 2 cups grated & packed lightly)
1 cup baby food carrots (four 4-ounce jars)
1 teaspoon ground mace
1 teaspoon cinnamon
1/8 teaspoon cloves
1/2 cup heavy cream

> Stir **mace, cinnamon** and **cloves** into heavy **cream**

Beat cream cheese in large mixing bowl on low speed about 5 minutes, until smooth and shiny; scrape 2-3 times. Add sugar and beat on low for 2-3 minutes, scraping at least once. With mixer on low, shake flour over batter and beat in. Increase speed one notch and beat 3-4 minutes, scraping several times.

At slow speed again, add eggs one at a time, beating well after each. Scrape gently after 2nd and 4th eggs, then beat on medium-low for 2 minutes. With mixer back on low, add baby food carrots and mix several minutes. Scrape once or twice to be sure carrots are mixed in well. Add cream and spice mixture slowly; mix for another 3-4 minutes. Add grated carrots and vanilla, beat 2 more minutes or until mixed thoroughly. Filling should be consistent in color and texture. Lift beaters and let drip back into bowl.

Pour into 3 prepared 6-inch cheesecake pans. Stir with spatula as you pour to keep carrots in the filling, not on the bottom of the bowl. Bake in preheated 400° oven for 15 minutes, then reduce heat to 325° and bake for 1 hour. Turn oven off and leave cheesecakes in for 2-3 hours, or until pans are comfortable to touch. This is a soft, moist cheesecake so it would be ok with an extra fifteen minutes cooking time, if preferred. ♥Refrigerate, Room, Release, Serve, Store♥

Notes: This recipe is like tuna fish and potato salad—each person has a distinct preference, usually for his or her own. My first attempt was with regular-sized carrots (grated) and mace. Some liked the texture of the carrots and some didn't. One-Man thought it was bland; he was really congested, though, so who knows. Cynthia thought it was nearly too strong, but liked the carrot texture; then she decided the taste was not too strong. She's tasted several versions and is sticking with carrot texture. Lisa, said "mmm, this tastes like Christmas." Jack liked the taste of the second version better, but preferred no carrot texture. This recipe was my second try, and I'm pretty happy with it.

Christmas Cheesecake: use mace as the sole spice. Actually, you could make this one without the carrots. Simply add mace to Just Plain Great recipe.

Frosting

1 8-ounce package cream cheese, room temperature
1 package (16-ounce) confectioners' sugar
1 tsp vanilla

Mix cream cheese to soften, add vanilla. Slowly add sugar and mix on low until smooth. Spread on cheesecake. Yield: 2-1/2 cups.

Notes: Carrot cake cheesecake seems to appeal to people (especially men, for some reason) who aren't dessert-crazy but do like carrot cake. Because there are so many ways to vary it, and it is so rich, this has great potential to become your signature dessert.

Cheesecake Light

This has a few less calories, but is by no means calorie-free. To me, it's better to have a small amount of the real thing, but this definitely works. Calories can be adjusted by changing amounts or regular, no fat, light and Neufchâtel.

<u>All cream cheese should be at room temperature</u>
1 (8-ounce) package cream cheese, regular
2 (8-ounce) packages cream cheese, no-fat
3 (8-ounce) packages "light" or "1/3 less" cream cheese
    or Neufchâtel*
3/4 cup granulated sugar
1/3 cup all-purpose flour
4 large eggs, room temperature
1 cup heavy cream, room temperature
1 cup fat free half-and-half, room temperature*
1-1/2 tablespoons vanilla

"Light" crust recipe is on page 48.

Beat cream cheese in large mixing bowl on low speed about 5 minutes, until smooth and shiny; scrape 2-3 times. Add sugar and beat on low for 2-3 minutes, scraping at least once. With mixer on low, shake flour over batter and beat in. Increase speed one notch and beat 3-4 minutes, scraping several times.

At low speed again, add eggs one at a time; beat well after each. Scrape gently after 2nd and 4th eggs, then beat on medium-low for 2 minutes. With mixer back on low, add heavy cream and half-and-half slowly; mix for another 3-4 minutes. Add vanilla, beat 2 more minutes. Lift beaters and let drip back into bowl. Pour into 3 prepared 6-inch cheesecake pans. Bake in preheated 400° oven for 15 minutes, then reduce heat to 300° for 1 hour. Turn oven off and leave cheesecakes in for 2-3 hours, or until pans are comfortable to touch. ♥Refrigerate, Room, Release, Serve, Store♥

Notes: *This is a heavy filling but low volume; add another 1/2 cup half-and-half if preferred, either regular or fat free. These cheesecakes probably will crack. The lower fat ingredients are a different consistency. Try baking at 300° for 75 minutes, rather than setting at higher temperature initially.
Another baking option: 400° for 10 minutes and then 325° for just 45 minutes.
    *Neufchâtel cheese and "light" or "1/3 less fat light" cream cheese are essentially the same thing. Take a minute to read labels.
    Page 119 shows a typical comparison of "real" and "low-fat" calories. However, it is not based on the exact recipes in this book. Calorie counts vary with brand. In addition, obviously, this recipe can be made lighter by using more "no-fat" cream cheese, less heavy cream and more fat free half-and-half, etc.

Chocolate Chip

This one tastes like creamy chocolate chip cookies. You can have chips sink to the bottom for a layer of chocolate, or have them "float" throughout the filling. Even using light brown sugar, rather than dark, this is a VERY rich dessert. Delicious with a cup of smooth coffee. FYI, the correct baking term for chip is morsel. But it just doesn't have the same ring, does it?

3 pounds cream cheese, room temperature
2 cups brown sugar, light or dark or combination
1/3 cup all-purpose flour
4 large eggs, room temperature
1 cup heavy cream, room temperature
1/2 cup half-and-half, room temperature
1-1/2 cups (12-ounce bag) semisweet chips (morsels)
1 tablespoon vanilla

Beat cream cheese in large mixing bowl on low speed about 5 minutes, until smooth and shiny; scrape 2-3 times. Add brown sugar and beat on low for 2-3 minutes, scraping at least once. With mixer on low, shake flour over batter and beat in. Increase speed one notch and beat 3-4 minutes, scraping several times.

At slow speed again, add eggs one at a time, beating well after each. Scrape after 2nd and 4th eggs, then beat on medium-low for 2 minutes. With mixer back on low, add heavy cream and half-and-half slowly and mix for another 3-4 minutes. Add vanilla, beat 2 more minutes. On low, stir in chocolate chips. Lift beaters and let drip back into bowl. See notes!

Pour into 3 prepared 6-inch cheesecake pans. Bake in preheated 400° oven for 15 minutes, then reduce heat to 325° for 1 hour. Turn oven off and leave cheesecakes in for 2-3 hours, or until pans are comfortable to touch. ♥Refrigerate, Room, Release, Serve, Store♥

Notes: Mixing chips in with the mixer makes them electromagnetic and they clump together. Experiment. An option is to fold in chips with rubber spatula.

Chocolate chips settle on the bottom of the cheesecake during cooking. The cheesecake will have a layer of chocolate on top of the crust. It will look like you did it on purpose. People will be impressed.

If you **coat the chips with flour first**, and mix in with mixer or by hand, fewer will settle to the bottom. Experiment with different-sized chips, or mix large and small chips, until you find what you like.

You can omit chips from filling, pour in 1/3 to 1/2 of the filling, add chocolate chips, pour more filling, add more chips. Distribution is more even that way, theoretically. Usually, I'm too impatient to take the extra time and it doesn't work for me.

For presentation, remember you have to cut through the chips. A giant chocolate kiss, wrapped or unwrapped, on top of each slice would be pretty.

68

Chocolate Nut

Potential decadence here, especially with chocolate nut crust..

3 pounds cream cheese, room temperature
1-1/2 cups granulated sugar
1/3 cup all-purpose flour
4 large eggs, room temperature
8 ounces unsweetened chocolate, melted
1 cup heavy cream, room temperature
1 cup half-and-half, room temperature
1 cup pecans, coarse pieces
1 cup blanched almonds, coarse pieces
2 teaspoons vanilla

1. Melt **chocolate,** heavy **cream** and **half-and-half** in heavy pan over LOW heat. COOL. *

2. Beat cream cheese in large mixing bowl on low speed about 5 minutes, until smooth and shiny; scrape 2-3 times. Add sugar and beat on low for 2-3 minutes, scraping at least once. With mixer on low, shake flour over batter and beat in flour. Increase speed one notch and beat 3-4 minutes, scraping several times.

At slow speed again, add eggs one at a time, beating well after each. Scrape after 2nd and 4th eggs, then beat on medium-low for 2 minutes.

3. With mixer back on low, add chocolate mixture (step 1) slowly and mix for another 3-4

minutes *OR, **add 1 to 2 cups of filling to pan with chocolate mixture** and stir well by hand. Then, add this chocolate mixture to filling in mixing bowl and beat thoroughly.

Adding chocolate directly to the filling may make the texture speckled, but doesn't change the taste; this recipe has so many nuts it probably doesn't matter.

4. Add all the nuts and vanilla, beat 2 more minutes. Lift beaters and let drip back into bowl.

Pour into 3 prepared 6-inch cheesecake pans, stirring with spatula as you pour to keep nuts evenly distributed. Bake in preheated 400° oven for 15 minutes, then reduce heat to 300° for 75 minutes. Turn oven off and leave cheesecakes in for 2-3 hours, or until pans are comfortable to touch. ♥Refrigerate, Room, Release, Serve, Store♥

Notes: This may crack a little, so remember: slow beating and no peeking.

Chocolate Swirl

This is a gorgeous sight. Plus, when you cut it, the chocolate aroma floats up to warm you like an unexpected smile, or a spontaneous hug from a good friend.

3 pounds cream cheese, room
    temperature
1-1/2 cups granulated sugar
1/3 cup all-purpose flour
4 large eggs, room temperature
8 ounces unsweetened chocolate
2/3 cup heavy cream, room
    temperature
1/3 cup half-and-half
1/3 cup granulated sugar
1/2 cup heavy cream,
    room temperature + 1 tablespoon vanilla for plain
    filling (step 4)
1/2 cup heavy cream, room temperature + 1 teaspoon
    vanilla for chocolate filling (step 5)

1. Melt **chocolate** in **2/3 cup** heavy **cream, 1/3 half-and-half** and **1/3 cup sugar** in heavy pan over LOW heat. Stir occasionally. It's thick. COOL. Add 2 cups plain filling and mix very well. See * (#3.)

    2. Beat cream cheese in large mixing bowl on low speed about 5 minutes, scrape 2-3 times. Add 1-1/2 cups sugar and beat on low for 2-3 minutes, scraping at least once.

    With mixer on low, shake flour over batter and beat in. Increase speed one notch and beat 3-4 minutes, scraping several times. At slow speed again, add eggs one at a time, beating well after each; scrape gently after 2nd and 4th eggs, then beat on medium-low for 2 minutes.

3.* Spoon about 2 cups of plain batter into the chocolate mixture and stir well. You can mix by hand or with mixer. A milk warmer is great for this. You can melt the chocolate in it and then add the filling and stir. KEEP FILLING IN SEPARATE BOWLS.

4. Add 1/2 cup heavy cream and 1 tablespoon vanilla to plain mixture and mix well AND

5. Add 1/2 cup heavy cream and 1 teaspoon vanilla to chocolate mixture and mix well.

6. Swirl or marble however you'd prefer. See page 94 for detailed directions. It's part of the art. Have fun.

Bake at 400° for 15 minutes, reduce oven to 300° and bake for 75 minutes. Turn oven off and leave cheesecakes in oven with door closed for 2-3 hours, or until pans are comfortable to touch. ♥Refrigerate, Room, Release, Serve, Store♥

Notes: Remember, the fillings need to be the same consistency to reduce fault lines (cracks), so add half-and-half or cream to the thicker one (probably the chocolate).

This one mellows wonderfully, and as stated, is visually pleasing. It definitely has fancy dessert possibilities.

Cocoa

Smells delicious! This is really easy because it uses cocoa powder—no chocolate to melt. It's a dark chocolate pudding kind of thing.

3 pounds cream cheese, room temperature
1-1/2 cups granulated sugar
1/3 cup all-purpose flour
1 cup cocoa powder
4 large eggs, room temperature
1 cup heavy cream, room temperature
1 cup half-and-half, room temperature
1 tablespoon vanilla (Mexican vanilla is good here)

Beat cream cheese in large mixing bowl on low speed about 5 minutes, until smooth and shiny; scrape 2-3 times. Add sugar and beat on low for 2-3 minutes, scraping at least once. With mixer on low, shake flour over batter and beat well. Stop mixer. Add cocoa slowly, but all at once; start on slow speed to avoid cocoa powder "clouds." Increase speed to medium-low and beat until light uniform color—no streaks. Small lumps or bumps are ok. Scrape occasionally.

At slow speed again, add eggs one at a time; beat thoroughly after each. Scrape after 2nd and 4th eggs, then beat on medium-low for 2 minutes. With mixer back on low, add heavy cream and half-and-half slowly and mix for another 3-4 minutes. Add vanilla, beat 2 more minutes. Lift beaters and let drip back into bowl.

Pour into 3 prepared 6-inch cheesecake pans. Bake in preheated 400° oven for 15 minutes, then reduce heat to 325° and bake for 1 hour. Turn oven off and leave cheesecakes in for 2-3 hours, or until pans are comfortable to touch. ♥Refrigerate, Room, Release, Serve, Store♥

Notes: Cheesecakes with cocoa powder are prone to cracking, so avoid opening the oven door until time to take them out. If cracking is a consistent problem, try lowering the oven temperature 15 degrees and extending baking time by 15 minutes. Just keep notes, and when you hit the right combination, use it.

Coconut

This gets fantastic raves from coconut lovers. It's smooth, creamy and moist. Great with hot chocolate sauce.

3 pounds cream cheese, room temperature
1 cup granulated sugar
1/3 cup all-purpose flour
4 large eggs, room temperature
1 cup sweetened coconut
1 cup unsweetened coconut
1 cup heavy cream, room temperature
1 cup coconut milk, room temperature
1 tablespoon vanilla, if desired

Beat cream cheese in large mixing bowl on low speed about 5 minutes, until smooth and shiny; scrape 2-3 times. Add sugar and beat on low for 2-3 minutes, scraping at least once. With mixer on low, shake flour over batter and beat in. Increase speed one notch and beat 3-4 minutes, scraping several times.

At low speed again, add eggs one at a time, beating well after each. Scrape gently after 2nd and 4th eggs, then beat on medium-low for 2 minutes. With mixer back on low, add heavy cream and coconut milk slowly; mix for another 3-4 minutes. Add vanilla, if desired, and coconut. Beat 2-3 more minutes, or until coconut is evenly dispersed. Coconut may be folded in with a spatula. Lift beaters and let drip into bowl.

Pour into 3 prepared 6-inch cheesecake pans. Stir with spatula as you pour, if necessary, to keep coconut mixed. Bake in preheated 400° oven for 15 minutes, then reduce heat to 325° and bake for 1 hour. Turn oven off and leave in for 2-3 hours, or until pans are comfortable to touch. ♥Refrigerate, Room, Release, Serve, Store♥

Notes: This really is delicious. Using a combination of shredded and flaked coconut (see "Other Stuff" on page 29) gives a uniform texture that is pleasing to the eye and the palate. However, use whatever you like, or have on hand, sweetened or unsweetened, shredded or flaked.

Naples Grape Festival Grape

The Finger Lakes region of New York is breath-taking in the fall. I developed this cheesecake to sell at the Naples Grape Festival in Naples, New York. The filling is a pleasing light purple but bakes to a light golden brown. The grape aroma is great during baking. Surprisingly, most people like this one. For fun, don't tell them what it is and see who can guess correctly.

3 pounds cream cheese, room temperature
4 large eggs, room temperature
1 cup granulated sugar
1/3 cup all-purpose flour
1 to 1-1/2 cups (16- or 18-ounce jar is ok) grape jam*
1/4 cup purple grape juice
1/4 cup heavy cream, room temperature
1/2 teaspoon grape oil

Beat cream cheese in large mixing bowl on low speed about 5 minutes, until smooth and shiny; scrape 2-3 times. Add sugar and beat on low for 2-3 minutes, scraping at least once. With mixer on low, shake flour over batter and beat until well mixed. Increase speed one notch and beat 3-4 minutes, scraping several times.

At slow speed again, add eggs one at a time, beating well after each. Scrape gently after 2nd and 4th eggs, then beat on medium-low for 2 minutes. With mixer back on low, add jam. When completely mixed, add grape juice slowly. Finally, add heavy cream and grape oil, and mix for another 3-4 minutes. Add vanilla, beat 2 more minutes. Lift beaters and let drip back into bowl.

Pour into 3 prepared 6-inch cheesecake pans. Bake in preheated 400° oven for 15 minutes, then reduce heat to 300° for 90 minutes. Turn oven off and leave in for 2-3 hours, or until pans are comfortable to touch. ♥Refrigerate, Room, Release, Serve, Store♥.

Notes: It's definitely an acquired taste, but If you're ever in a grape part of the country and have a chance, try a piece of grape pie, with or without a scoop of vanilla ice cream.

*16-ounce jar = about 1-1/3 cups
18-ounce jar = about 1-1/2 cups

Peanut Butter & Jam Swirl

This is a great "and now for something a little different" dessert.

3 pounds cream cheese, room temperature
1-1/4 cups granulated sugar
1/3 cup all-purpose flour
4 large eggs, room temperature
1-1/2 cups (18 ounce jar) jam or preserves, your choice
1-1/2 cups (18 ounce jar) peanut butter, your choice *
1 cup total heavy cream, room temperature
1 cup total half-and-half, room temperature

Beat cream cheese in large mixing bowl on low speed about 5 minutes, until smooth and shiny; scrape 2-3 times. Add sugar and beat on low for 2-3 minutes, scraping at least once. With mixer on low, shake flour over batter and mix. Increase speed one notch and beat 3-4 minutes, scraping several times. At slow speed again, add eggs one at a time, beating well after each. Scrape after 2nd and 4th eggs, then beat on medium-low for 2 minutes.

Divide filling in half. To one half, add the jam or preserves <u>AND</u> 1/2 cup heavy cream and 1/2 cup half-and-half. To other half, add peanut butter <u>AND</u> 1/2 cup heavy cream and 1/2 cup half-and-half. If one portion is much thicker than the other, add more cream or half-and-half to the thicker one. Cooking will be more uniform, and chances of cracking will be reduced if the fillings are the same consistency.

OR: Add the peanut butter, 1/2 cup cream and 1/2 cup half-and-half to all the filling. Then divide into two portions and add the jam or preserves, 1/2 cup cream and 1/2 cup half-and-half to one-half of the mixture.

OR: Just dump everything in the same bowl, mix and pour! This eliminates swirling, of course.

Swirl (page 94) however you'd like and pour into 3 prepared 6-inch cheesecake pans. Bake in preheated 400° oven for 15 minutes, then reduce heat to 325° for 1 hour; then reduce heat to 275° for 15 minutes. Turn oven off, leave door closed for 15-30 minutes, then barely crack oven door and let cool for 2-3 hours, or until pans are comfortable to touch. ♥Refrigerate, Room, Release, Serve, Store♥

Notes: This makes a lot of filling. (Reduce volume by using just 1 cup each of jam and peanut butter.) It is enough for one 9-inch wide by 3-inch high pan and about 1/2 of a 6-inch pan. Three 6-inch pans will be full. These may crack where the different fillings meet. They look beautiful cooking, and come out a nice golden brown. A dark-colored jam will give more contrast, which is nice when you cut the cheesecake.

*Unless you really like salty food, try this one with unsalted or low-salt peanut butter the first time. Smooth or crunchy is a personal preference choice.

Pineapple

This is a great combo of cool and creamy with just a bit of pineapple tang. Superb choice in summer, if I do say so myself.

3 pounds cream cheese, room temperature
1-1/4 cups granulated sugar
1/3 cup all-purpose flour
4 large eggs, room temperature
1 cup heavy cream
1/4 cup half-and-half
1/2 cup juice (liquid from can)
2 (20-ounce) cans crushed unsweetened pineapple,
    well-drained

Beat cream cheese in large mixing bowl on low speed about 5 minutes, until smooth and shiny; scrape 2-3 times. Add sugar and beat on low for 2-3 minutes, scraping at least once. With mixer on low, shake flour over batter and beat in. Increase speed one notch and beat 3-4 minutes, scraping several times.

At slow speed again, beat in eggs one at a time. Scrape after 2nd and 4th eggs, then beat on medium-low for 2 minutes. With mixer back on low, beat in heavy cream and half-and-half. Add pineapple juice slowly and mix for another 3-4 minutes. Beat in pineapple. Lift beaters and let drip back into bowl.

Pour into 3 prepared 6-inch cheesecake pans. Bake in preheated 400° oven for 15 minutes, then

reduce heat to 300° for 75 to 90 minutes. Turn oven off and leave cheesecakes in oven with door closed for 2-3 hours, or until pans are comfortable to touch.
♥Refrigerate, Room, Release, Serve, Store♥

Notes: See page 114 for topping recipes. Not to overstate the obvious, but bigger chunks of pineapple will settle on the bottom. Crushed pineapple stays distributed more evenly but you don't get the same "pineapple experience." I think pulling apart slices into small chunks is best, but I don't always have the patience. It's another personal preference. This cheesecake has potential to get soggy, especially if pineapple isn't drained thoroughly; again, bigger chunks sitting on crust will have a higher "sog" potential.

This one is really tough to get a completely dry, pulled-in-perfectly-cleanly-from-the-sides look.

At times this is high on my favorite list. After it's mellowed, it tastes like a frozen pineapple dessert my mother made when we were really young. I think it had evaporated milk and lemon juice. She poured it in an ice tray to freeze. Who knows what I'm talking about? If you do, and have a recipe, please send it to me.

Pumpkin Pie

A "crossover!" This is one of my favorites—I just melt into the taste and smoothness. It smells and tastes delicious and looks beautiful cooked. Great made with ginger snap cookie crust. People who like pumpkin pie but not cheesecake, and those who like cheesecake but not pumpkin pie, may like pumpkin cheesecake. This has a really high "wow, this is fantastic" response.

3 pounds cream cheese, room temperature
1-1/4 cups granulated sugar
1/3 cup all-purpose flour
4 large eggs, room temperature
1 large (29 ounces) can Libby's® Pumpkin
2 teaspoons cinnamon
1 teaspoon cloves   Stir spices into pumpkin
1 teaspoon ginger
1/2 cup heavy cream, room
    temperature   Evaporated milk may be
                         substituted here if
1/2 cup half-and-half, room   preferred, but why?
    temperature

Beat cream cheese in large mixing bowl on low speed about 5 minutes, until smooth and shiny; scrape 2-3 times. Add sugar and beat on low for 2-3 minutes, scraping at least once. <u>Do not get this batter too fluffy—low speeds are better</u>. With mixer on low, shake flour over batter. Beat 3-4 minutes, scraping several times.

Add eggs one at a time, beating well after each. Scrape after 2nd and 4th eggs, then beat on medium-low for 2 minutes. On low speed, add pumpkin and spices; beat 3-4 minutes, until pumpkin is thoroughly mixed. Add heavy cream and half-and-half and beat until mixed into filling. It will take a few minutes. The color should be uniform. Lift beaters and let drip back into bowl.

Pour into 3 prepared 6-inch cheesecake pans. Pans will be very full! Bake in preheated 400° oven for 15 minutes, then reduce heat to 300° for 75 minutes. Turn oven off, leave door closed and let sit for two or three hours, or until pans are comfortable to touch. ♥Refrigerate, Room, Release, Serve, Store♥

Notes: This is a soft cheesecake, so experiment with cooking temperatures and times. If the pans are really full, and you expand cooking time, puff odds increase. I actually had one "explode" and blow part of it's top! Didn't effect the taste, and it was funny. I blamed it on Lisa, because I kept opening the oven on a Texas blue-norther kind of day to demonstrate visual hints. Make a firmer cheesecake by omitting cream or half-and-half, or both. This also eliminates a few calories, but defeats total indulgence! This cheesecake is great, great, great for Thanksgiving! Make it a few days in advance, and serve it at just about room temperature, with smooth, rich, dark coffee. Share with a special friend!

Raspberry

3 pounds cream cheese, room temperature
1 cup granulated sugar
1/3 cup all-purpose flour
4 large eggs, room temperature
1 to 1-1/2 cups raspberry jam or preserves*
1 cup heavy cream, room temperature
1 cup half-and-half, room temperature
1 tablespoon vanilla

Beat cream cheese in large mixing bowl on low speed about 5 minutes, until smooth and shiny; scrape 2-3 times. Add sugar and beat on low for 2-3 minutes, scraping at least once. With mixer on low, shake flour over batter and beat in. Increase speed one notch and beat 3-4 minutes, scraping several times.

At slow speed again, add eggs one at a time; beat well after each. Scrape after 2nd and 4th eggs, then beat on medium-low for 2 minutes. With mixer back on low, add jam and blend in; add heavy cream, half-and-half and vanilla slowly and mix for another 3-4 minutes. Lift beaters and let drip back into bowl.

Pour into 3 prepared 6-inch cheesecake pans. Put in preheated 400° oven for 15 minutes, then reduce heat to 325° for 1 hour. Turn oven off, leave cheesecakes in oven with door closed for 2-3 hours, or until pans are comfortable to touch. ♥Refrigerate, Room, Release, Serve, Store♥➙➙

Strawberry

3 pounds cream cheese, room temperature
1 cup granulated sugar
1/3 cup all-purpose flour
4 large eggs, room temperature
1 to 1-1/2 cups strawberry jam or preserves*
1 cup heavy cream, room temperature
1 cup half-and-half, room temperature
1 tablespoon vanilla

➡Notes: Obviously, the difference in these two recipes is jam. Experiment with your own favorites—blackberry, blueberry, etc. Jam or preserves work, but jelly probably isn't as good a choice. Seeds or seedless is a consideration, obviously. Use homemade jam if available.

*One cup of jam is enough, but an 18-ounce jar is about a cup and a half. If I'm not going to reserve some for topping, I just dump in the whole jar. Otherwise, I end up with a refrigerator full of jars.

Presentation could be plain, but also might include fresh fruit, or preserves, or a warm or cold sauce. Fruit or chocolate sauces are considerations. See the Toppings section (page 114), or another source, or make up your own. Chocolate-dipped berries would be pretty, maybe with a mint leaf or two.

Strawberry Chocolate

This cheesecake bakes nicely in a 9- or 10-inch pan. It's firm and easy to handle. And rich!

3 pounds cream cheese, room
  temperature
1-1/2 cups granulated sugar
1/3 cup all-purpose flour
4 large eggs, room temperature
8 ounces unsweetened chocolate
1-1/2 cups (18-ounce jar)
  strawberry jam or preserves*
1-1/2 cups heavy cream, room
  temperature
1-2 teaspoons vanilla

1. In milk warmer or heavy pan, melt **chocolate** over LOW heat; stir frequently. Take off heat, cool briefly, stir in **jam** and heavy **cream**; mix well. COOL. Add 2 cups **filling** and mix thoroughly.

2. Beat cream cheese in large mixing bowl on low speed about 5 minutes, until smooth and shiny; scrape 2-3 times. Add sugar and beat on low for 2-3 minutes, scraping at least once. With mixer on low, shake flour over batter and beat in. Increase speed one notch and beat 3-4 minutes; scrape frequently. At slow speed again, add eggs one at a time, beating well after each. Scrape after 2nd and 4th eggs, then beat on medium-low for 2 minutes.

3. With mixer back on low, add chocolate mixture (step 1) and beat until completely mixed.

Add vanilla and beat 2 more minutes. Lift beaters and let drip back into bowl.

    4. Pour into 3 prepared 6-inch cheesecake pans. Bake in preheated 400° oven for 15 minutes, then reduce heat to 325° for 1 hour. Turn oven off and leave in closed oven 2-3 hours, or until pans are comfortable to touch. ♥Refrigerate, Room, Release, Serve, Store♥

    Notes: <u>Start the chocolate mixture first; otherwise, you'll end up waiting for it to melt and cool.</u>

    You can add the cooled chocolate, jam and cream mixture from step 1 directly to the filling, but you might get speckles. Taste doesn't change, though.

    *One cup of jam or preserves is enough; that would leave 1/2 cup for topping (see page 114). It's a seed versus seedless choice, also. Homemade jam is great to use, if available.

    A very small dab of strawberry preserves, or a fresh strawberry or two on each slice would be great. Or a chocolate-dipped strawberry. Or a strawberry nestled in chocolate curls—you get the idea.

    Fillings with chocolate are more sensitive to puffing and cracking,so keep peeking to a minimum.

Sugar-Free

Over the years, requests have been made to develop a no-sugar cheesecake. I've always resisted, because, personally, I think it's better to eat a tiny bit of the real thing. Also, I'm not sure artificial sweetener is any better for us than sugar. However, I know that choice is not always an option. This cheesecake is best eaten the day after it is made.

3 pounds cream cheese, room temperature
3 large eggs, room temperature
1 cup Equal® artificial sweetener
1/4 cup all-purpose flour
1 cup heavy cream, room temperature
1/2 cup half-and-half, room temperature
1 to 2 tablespoons vanilla

Crust: Butter pans, dust with crushed crackers, put in oven until warm, shake excess crumbs off.

Beat cream cheese in large mixing bowl on low speed about 5 minutes, until smooth and shiny; scrape 2-3 times. Add sweetener and beat on low for 2-3 minutes, scraping at least once. With mixer on low, shake flour over batter and beat in flour. Increase speed one notch and beat 3-4 minutes, scraping several times.

At slow speed again, add eggs one at a time, beating well after each. Scrape after 2nd and 4th eggs, then beat on medium-low for 2 minutes. With mixer back on low, add heavy cream and half-and-half slowly and mix for another 3-4 minutes. Add vanilla, beat 2 more minutes. Lift beaters and let drip back into bowl. Do not scrape beaters into bowl—large chunks will stay that way.

Pour into 3 prepared 6-inch cheesecake pans. Bake in preheated 375° oven for 30 minutes, then reduce heat to 325° for 20 minutes, and then reduce to 300° for 30-35 minutes. Turn oven off and cool in closed oven 2-3 hours, or until pans are comfortable to touch. ♥Refrigerate, Room, Release, Serve, Store♥

Notes: Comes out of pans easier when nearly room temperature. You can use regular crust recipe and omit sugar, but it's pretty "thick."

Sweet (German) Chocolate

This may be more familiar as "German Chocolate." Really, it's Baker's® German's® Brand Sweet Chocolate Bar.

3 pounds cream cheese, room
   temperature
1 to 1-1/4 cups granulated sugar
1/3 cup all-purpose flour
4 large eggs, room temperature
4 ounces sweet chocolate
   ("German chocolate")
1 cup cream, room temperature
1 cup half-and-half,
   room temperature
1 tablespoon vanilla

1. Melt **chocolate** in heavy **cream** and **half-and-half** over LOW heat. COOL. Add 1-2 cups **filling**, mix well, and return all to mixing bowl.*

2. Beat cream cheese in large mixing bowl on low speed about 5 minutes, until smooth and shiny; scrape 2-3 times. Add sugar and beat on low for 2-3 minutes, scraping at least once. With mixer on low, shake flour over batter and beat well. Increase speed one notch and beat 3-4 minutes, scraping several times.

3. At slow speed again, add eggs one at a time, beating well after each. Scrape after 2nd and 4th eggs, then beat on medium-low for 2 minutes.

4. With mixer back on low, add chocolate and heavy cream mixture slowly and mix for another 3-4 minutes **OR*** add 1 to 2 cups of the filling to the

chocolate mixture, and stir well by hand. Then, add chocolate mixture to filling in bowl and beat thoroughly. Adding chocolate and cream to all of the filling may make the texture speckled, but doesn't change the taste. Add vanilla, beat 2 more minutes. Lift beaters and let drip back into bowl.

    5. Pour into 3 prepared 6-inch cheesecake pans. Bake in preheated 400° oven for 15 minutes, then reduce heat to 325° for 1 hour. Turn oven off and leave cheesecakes in for 2-3 hours, or until pans are comfortable to touch. ♥Refrigerate, Room, Release, Serve, Store♥

    Presentation: Serve with Coconut Pecan Topping (page 117). Here's a personal confession for all of you who think I never gorge, or binge, or eat sugar; I eat this topping with a spoon—forget the cheesecake!

White Chocolate with Macadamia

This is worth trying. The first bite or two are good, but then about bite number three the white chocolate taste explodes in your mouth. Then the undercurrent of macadamia nuts surfaces. It is so good! Another serendipity—really, it was supposed to be white chocolate and almond, because that is Bruce's favorite ice cream. But he said this was ok. And, to my brother, Phil, in Bakersfield: I decided not to put in what you said Bill said about this cheesecake. So, you owe me big time. Bill, you and Lucinda should know better than to tell Phil not to tell. He never could keep a secret.

3 pounds cream cheese,
    room temperature
1 cup granulated sugar
1/3 cup all-purpose flour
4 large eggs, room
    temperature

1. Melt **2 cups chips** with heavy **cream** and **half-and-half** in heavy pan over LOW heat. Stir occasionally. COOL.

1 cup heavy cream, room temperature
1 cup half-and-half, room temperature
2 cups white chocolate chips to melt with liquids
1 cup white chocolate chips to add to filling
1 cup chopped macadamia nuts
1 teaspoon vanilla, if desired

2. Beat cream cheese in large mixing bowl on low speed about 5 minutes, until smooth and shiny; scrape 2-3 times. Add sugar and beat on low for 2-3 minutes, scraping at least once. With mixer on low, shake flour

over batter and beat in. Increase speed one notch and beat 3-4 minutes, scraping several times.

3. At low speed again, add eggs one at a time; beat well after each. Scrape after 2nd and 4th eggs. After last egg, scrape and then beat on medium-low for 2 minutes.

4. With mixer back on low, add cooled white chocolate mixture to the filling in the mixing bowl. Add vanilla, if desired, and beat 2-3 minutes. Lift beaters and let drip back into bowl.

5. Fold in 1 cup chips and the nuts with a rubber spatula.

6. Pour into 3 prepared 6-inch cheesecake pans. Bake in preheated 400° oven for 15 minutes, then reduce heat to 325° for 1 hour. Turn oven off and cool in closed oven 2-3 hours, or until pans are comfortable to touch. ♥Refrigerate, Room, Release, Serve, Store♥

Notes: Remember to <u>start white chocolate mixture first</u>, so you don't have to sit and wait for it to cool.

Variations

♦ Gee, how about almonds instead of macadamia nuts?
♦ Or, chocolate chips in addition to the white?

SWIRL DIRECTIONS

For some reason, I occasionally find "'swirling" to be a pain. Of course, some days, just existing is a pain...anyway, there are several ways to swirl, or marble, cheesecakes. Really, it's part of the art.

The **consistency of the fillings needs to be the same**, so add half-and-half or cream to the thicker one if necessary. Chocolate and liqueur fillings dry out quicker than plain during baking. Think of where the batters meet as a fault line—cracking is more likely. First, <u>divide the filling</u> in half.

♥ Pour one bowl into the center of the other one. With a wide spatula, carefully fold the filling, going from the rim, down the side, across the bottom and up the other side two or three times. DO NOT STIR. Pour into pans.

♥ Pour one bowl into the center of other bowl. With spatula, go down the middle of the "poured" filling and bring it out the the edge of the bowl several times, like you're tracing spokes of a wheel from the hub to the rim. DO NOT STIR. Pour into pans.

♥ Pour fillings into pans in alternate layers, creating 3 or 4 layers. Gently run knife through the layers several times. Don't gauge the crust. Be creative, but DO NOT STIR.

Amaretto

3 pounds cream cheese, room temperature
1 cup granulated sugar
1/3 cup all-purpose flour
4 large eggs, room temperature
1 cup amaretto (almond-flavored liqueur)
1 cup heavy cream, room temperature
1 teaspoon almond extract <u>or</u> 1/4 teaspoon almond oil

Beat cream cheese in large mixing bowl on low speed about 5 minutes, until smooth and shiny; scrape 2-3 times. Add sugar and beat on low for 2-3 minutes, scraping at least once. With mixer on low, shake flour over batter and beat well. Increase speed one notch and beat 3-4 minutes, scraping several times.

At slow speed again, beat in eggs one at a time. Scrape after 2nd and 4th eggs, then beat on medium-low for 2 minutes. With mixer back on low, add heavy cream and amaretto slowly and mix for another 3-4 minutes. Add almond extract or oil, beat 2 more minutes. Lift beaters and let drip back into bowl.

Pour into 3 prepared 6-inch cheesecake pans. Put in preheated 400° oven for 15 minutes, then reduce heat to 325° for 1 hour. Turn oven off and leave cheesecakes in for 2-3 hours, or until pans are comfortable to touch. ♥Refrigerate, Room, Release, Serve, Store♥

Amaretto Coconut Almond

I sometimes order almonds from Ouida Marchant's family orchard in Terlock, California. "Fresh" almonds are incredible. If you're lucky enough to live in almond country, take advantage. They are awesome in the almond cookies I make. Actually, those cookies might make a good crust. Oh no, another experiment to perform.

3 pounds cream cheese, room temperature
1-1/4 cups granulated sugar
1/3 cup all-purpose flour
4 large eggs, room temperature
1 cup coconut milk
1 cup amaretto (almond-flavored liqueur)
1 cup coconut
1 cup almonds, blanched and chopped
1 teaspoon almond extract or 1/4 teaspoon almond oil
1 teaspoon vanilla

Beat cream cheese in large mixing bowl on low to medium speed about 5 minutes, until smooth and shiny; scrape 2-3 times. Add sugar and beat on low for 2-3 minutes, scraping at least once. With mixer on low, shake flour over batter and beat well. Increase speed one notch and beat 3-4 minutes, scraping several times.

At slow speed again, add eggs one at a time, beating well after each. Scrape after 2nd and 4th eggs, then beat on medium-low for 2 minutes. With mixer back on low, slowly add coconut milk and amaretto, mix for another 3-4 minutes. Add vanilla and almond extracts and beat 2 more minutes. Stir in coconut and almonds. Lift beaters and let drip back into bowl. You may need to fold as you pour.

Pour into 3 prepared 6-inch cheesecake pans. Bake in preheated 400° oven for 15 minutes, then reduce heat to 300° for 75 minutes. Turn oven off, cool in closed oven 2-3 hours, or until pans are comfortable to touch. ♥Refrigerate, Room, Release, Serve, Store♥

Notes: This is a good place to discuss efficient shopping and use of ingredients, as well as the flexibility of the recipes.

A good "six-pack" would be 3 Coconut and 3 Amaretto Coconut Almond, made at the same time. You have to get coconut out for both, and they both call for coconut milk. Each calls for 1 cup of coconut milk, but if it's a little short, just complete the cup with half-and-half, or split the coconut milk between the 2 recipes and complete each one with half-and-half.

To blanch almonds: Put whole almonds into boiling water for a few minutes, until skins loosen. Drain in colander and cool briefly. Press nut between thumb and forefinger to pop nut out of skin.

To toast almonds: heat in preheated 350° oven 5-7 minutes, stirring occasionally, until just browned. Baking sheet where nuts are just one layer thick works well. Toasting enhances the flavor, but is not required.

Bittersweet Chocolate

3 pounds cream cheese, room temperature
1 cup granulated sugar
1/3 cup all-purpose flour
4 large eggs, room temperature
8 ounces bittersweet chocolate
1 cup heavy cream,
  room temperature
1 cup chocolate liqueur
2 tablespoons vanilla
  (Mexican vanilla good here)

1. In milk warmer or heavy pan, melt **chocolate** in heavy **cream** over LOW heat until melted. COOL. Stir in 2 cups **filling**, mix well and add to mixer bowl.

2. Beat cream cheese in large mixing bowl on low speed about 5 minutes, until smooth and shiny; scrape 2-3 times. Add sugar and beat on low for 2-3 minutes, scraping at least once. With mixer on low, shake flour over batter and beat well. Increase speed one notch and beat 3-4 minutes, scraping several times. At slow speed again, add eggs one at a time; beat well after each. Scrape after 2nd and 4th eggs, then beat on medium-low for 2 minutes.

3. Take 2 cups of plain filling from mixing bowl and stir it into the cooled chocolate and cream mixture. Mix it well, using a spoon or spatula. Then, put the new chocolate mixture into the mixing bowl and mix on low.

4. Add liqueur slowly and mix for another 3-4 minutes. Add vanilla, beat 2 more minutes. Lift beaters and let drip back into bowl.

5. Pour into 3 prepared 6-inch cheesecake pans. Bake in preheated 400° oven for 15 minutes, then reduce heat to 325° for 1 hour. Turn oven off and cool in closed oven 2-3 hours, or until pans are comfortable to touch. ♥Refrigerate, Room, Release, Serve, Store♥

Notes: If you have trouble with this one cracking, try baking at 400° for 15 minutes, and then 75 minutes at 300°.

Remember to **start the chocolate** first. To avoid using double boiler, it needs to be melted slowly in a heavy pan, so it takes a while. Don't forget about it like I always do. It's a thick mixture, and will get thicker when you accidentally let it boil. Don't panic—just add extra cream or half-and-half to thin it down a little. It's another "art of making cheesecake" deal. You can add the cooled chocolate and cream mixture directly to the filling but you might get a speckled appearance. Taste will be ok, and you might like speckles, so just do what feels right.

Bittersweet Chocolate Raspberry Jam

10-21-90: For Halloween party. This is the most-requested flavor. When I lived in upstate New York, it was made with raspberry jam I made with raspberries I picked. If you have not tried picking raspberries, I recommend it at least once. For one thing, you'll appreciate why they are so expensive. For another, you'll taste the difference in "straight-off-the-vine" versus out of the grocery store. There's no comparison. Mostly, it's a great way to spend a few hours with a spouse or a friend or a neighbor, especially on temperate days with blue sky and yellow sunshine.

3 pounds cream cheese, room temperature
1 cup granulated sugar
1/3 cup all-purpose flour
4 large eggs, room temperature
8 ounces bittersweet chocolate
1 cup raspberry jam (up to 1-1/2
   cups ok)
1 cup heavy cream, room
   temperature
1 cup raspberry liqueur or crème
   de cassis
1 tablespoon vanilla

1. In milk warmer or heavy pan, melt **chocolate** over LOW heat, stirring frequently. COOL. Stir in 1-2 cups of **filling** and return to mixing bowl.*

2. Beat cream cheese in large mixing bowl on low speed about 5 minutes, until smooth and shiny; scrape 2-3 times. Add sugar and beat on low for 2-3 minutes, scraping at least once. With mixer on low, shake flour over filling and beat. Increase speed one notch and beat 3-4 minutes, scraping several times. At slow

speed again, add eggs one at a time, beating well after each. Scrape after 2nd and 4th eggs, then beat on medium-low for 2 minutes.

3. Stir 1 to 2 cups filling into cooled, melted chocolate (step 1), mix well, and return to mixer. Mix thoroughly at slow speed. Mix in jam, then add heavy cream and blend well. Add liqueur slowly and mix for another 3-4 minutes. Add vanilla, beat 2 more minutes. Lift beaters and let drip back into bowl.

4. Pour into 3 prepared 6-inch cheesecake pans. Bake in preheated 400° oven for 15 minutes, then reduce heat to 325° for 1 hour. Turn oven off and leave cheesecakes in for 2-3 hours, or until pans are comfortable to touch. ♥Refrigerate, Room, Release, Serve, Store♥

Notes: You can use up to 10 or 12 ounces of bittersweet chocolate. *If desired, melt chocolate in the cream, cool briefly, stir in the jam and liqueur, mix well, and then pour all of it into the mixer.

When I serve this at home, sometimes I put a very thin coat of raspberry preserves on top. If you're taking it to a gathering, it's easier to put the preserves on after you get there. Remember—the better the chocolate and preserves, the better the cheesecake.

If cracks are a problem, try 400° for 15 minutes and 300° for 75 minutes, or 300° for 90 minutes.

Crème de Cacao

This is a nice, smooth, easy taste. It needs a few days to mingle and mellow.

3 pounds cream cheese, room temperature
1-1/2 cups granulated sugar
1/3 cup all-purpose flour
1 cup cocoa powder (Dutch-process is great)
4 large eggs, room temperature
1 cup heavy cream, room temperature
1 cup crème de cacao liqueur
2 teaspoons vanilla (Mexican works well here)

Beat cream cheese in large mixing bowl on low speed about 5 minutes, until smooth and shiny; scrape 2-3 times. Add sugar and beat on low for 2-3 minutes, scraping at least once. With mixer on low, shake flour over batter and beat in. Turn mixer off and slowly add cocoa all at once; start mixer slowly to avoid getting cocoa-puffed. Beat 3-4 minutes, scraping several times. Don't worry about getting every single cocoa powder bump out.

At slow speed again, add eggs one at a time, beating well after each. Scrape after 2nd and 4th eggs, then beat on medium-low for 2 minutes. With mixer back on low, add heavy cream and liqueur slowly and mix for another 3-4 minutes. Add vanilla, beat 2 more minutes. Lift beaters and let drip back into bowl.

Pour into 3 prepared 6-inch cheesecake pans. Put in preheated 400° oven for 15 minutes, then reduce heat to 325° for 1 hour. Turn oven off and leave cheesecakes in for 2-3 hours, or until pans are comfortable to touch. ♥Refrigerate, Room, Release, Serve, Store♥

Notes: Don't get this one too fluffy—it'll crack for sure!

Crème de Menthe

I usually use green liqueur—it's fun to watch it swirl into the filling and it's a pretty color. It bakes to a golden brown, green on top, with green sides. It rises (puffs) a lot and therefore has a tendency to fall (sink), but usually doesn't crack. Cooking at a little lower temperature, maybe 300°, for 75 minutes is a consideration. This one keeps its kick!!

3 pounds cream cheese, room temperature
1-1/4 cups granulated sugar
1/3 cup all-purpose flour
4 large eggs, room temperature
1 cup heavy cream, room temperature
1 cup crème de menthe (green or white)
2 tablespoons vanilla

Beat cream cheese in large mixing bowl on low speed about 5 minutes, until smooth and shiny; scrape 2-3 times. Add sugar and beat on low for 2-3 minutes, scraping at least once. With mixer on low, shake flour over batter and beat in. Increase speed one notch and beat 3-4 minutes, scraping several times.

At slow speed again, add eggs one at a time, beating well after each. Scrape after 2nd and 4th eggs, then beat on medium-low for 2 minutes. With mixer back on low, add heavy cream and crème de menthe slowly and mix for another 3-4 minutes. Add vanilla, beat 2 more minutes. Lift beaters and let drip back into bowl.

Pour into 3 prepared 6-inch cheesecake pans. Bake in preheated 400° oven for 15 minutes, then reduce heat to 325°for 1 hour. Turn oven off and leave cheesecakes in for 2-3 hours, or until pans are comfortable to touch. ♥Refrigerate, Room, Release, Serve, Store♥

Notes: Chocolate drizzle, glaze or sauce would be nice presentation. See Toppings on page 116, or use your favorite recipe, or make up your own.

Variations

- Add 1 cup of grated bittersweet chocolate
- Add 1 or 2 cups of chocolate chips (morsels)
- Add 1 cup of cocoa powder
- Swirl melted chocolate through

Irish Cream

Smells delicious and is a really pleasing brown color. Plan on at least three days for this one to mellow, and, depending on your fire-in-the-gullet meter, a week may be more reasonable.

3 pounds cream cheese, room temperature
1-1/4 cups granulated sugar
1/3 cup all-purpose flour
4 large eggs, room temperature
1 cup heavy cream, room temperature
1 cup Irish Cream liqueur
2 teaspoons vanilla

Beat cream cheese in large mixing bowl on low speed about 5 minutes, until smooth and shiny; scrape 2-3 times. Add sugar and beat on low for 2-3 minutes, scraping at least once.

With mixer on low, shake flour over batter and beat until flour is incorporated. Increase speed one notch and beat 3-4 minutes, scraping several times.

At slow speed again, add eggs one at a time, beating well after each. Scrape after 2nd and 4th egg, then beat on medium-low for 2 minutes. With mixer back on low, add heavy cream and liqueur slowly and mix for another 3-4 minutes. Add vanilla, beat 2 more minutes. Lift beaters and let drip back into bowl. ➥ ➥

Kahlúa®

This is one recipe in which I use the name-brand, but use your favorite coffee liqueur. It holds its kick pretty well.

3 pounds cream cheese, room temperature
1-1/4 cups granulated sugar
1/3 cup all-purpose flour
4 large eggs, room temperature
1 cup heavy cream, room temperature
1 cup Kahlúa® or other coffee liqueur
2 teaspoons vanilla

→Pour into 3 prepared 6-inch cheesecake pans. Bake in preheated 400° oven for 15 minutes, then reduce heat to 325° for 1 hour. Turn oven off and leave cheesecakes in for 2-3 hours, or until pans are comfortable to touch. ♥Refrigerate, Room, Release, Serve, Store♥

Notes: Fillings with liqueur tend to crack a little easier. A baking option is 300° for 75 minutes. Less sugar may be necessary with a really sweet liqueur, but it's personal preference. These taste really good with a medium-strong coffee.

Peppermint with Chocolate Glaze

Cool cool cool! Refreshing! Zingy! Dark chocolate covering. Like biting into chocolate mint candy.

3 pounds cream cheese, room temperature
1 cup granulated sugar
1/3 cup all-purpose flour
4 large eggs, room temperature
1 cup heavy cream, room temperature
1 cup peppermint liqueur
1 teaspoon vanilla

Beat cream cheese in large mixing bowl on low speed about 5 minutes, until smooth and shiny; scrape 2-3 times. Add sugar and beat on low for 2-3 minutes, scraping at least once. With mixer on low, shake flour over batter and beat in. Increase speed one notch and beat 3-4 minutes, scraping several times.

At slow speed again, add eggs one at a time, beating well after each. Scrape after 2nd and 4th eggs, then beat on medium-low for 2 minutes. With mixer back on low, add heavy cream and peppermint liqueur slowly and mix for another 3-4 minutes. Add vanilla, beat 2 more minutes. Lift beaters and let drip back into bowl.

Pour into 3 prepared 6-inch cheesecake pans. Bake in preheated 400° oven for 15 minutes, then reduce heat to 325° for 1 hour. Turn oven off and leave cheesecakes in for 2-3 hours, or until pans are comfortable to touch. ♥Refrigerate, Room, Release, Serve, Store♥

Bittersweet Chocolate Glaze

8 ounces bittersweet chocolate, pieces or block
1/2 cup heavy cream

Melt together over low heat in heavy pan. Stir occasionally, until melted and completely smooth and blended. Cool briefly, spread over baked cheesecake and refrigerate briefly to set chocolate. Looks nice with chocolate drizzled over individual pieces also.

Notes: Any kind of chocolate will work; I just really like bittersweet chocolate to enhance the strong taste of peppermint. Milk chocolate might not be quite strong enough. Also, you can experiment with amounts of heavy cream to get the consistency you prefer.

Praline

Bakes to a beautiful light caramel color. For total indulgence, presentation could include a thin drizzle of warmed butter-pecan syrup. I usually forget, but substituting brown sugar in the crust and the filling is good, and very rich. This one keeps its intoxicating aroma and taste.

3 pounds cream cheese, room temperature
1-1/4 cups granulated sugar
1/3 cup all-purpose flour
4 large eggs, room temperature
1 cup heavy cream, room temperature
1 cup praline liqueur
1-1/2 cup chopped pecans

Beat cream cheese in large mixing bowl on low speed about 5 minutes, until smooth and shiny; scrape 2-3 times. Add sugar and beat on low for 2-3 minutes, scraping at least once. With mixer on low, shake flour over filling and beat in. Increase speed one notch and beat 3-4 minutes, scraping several times.

At slow speed again, add eggs one at a time, beating well after each. Scrape after 2nd and 4th eggs, then beat on medium-low for 2 minutes. With mixer back on low, add heavy cream and praline liqueur slowly and mix for another 3-4 minutes. Add vanilla, beat 2 more minutes. Lift beaters and let drip back into bowl. Fold in pecans with rubber spatula.

Pour into 3 prepared 6-inch cheesecake pans. Bake in preheated 400° oven for 15 minutes, then reduce heat to 300° for 75 minutes. Turn oven off and leave cheesecakes in for 2-3 hours, or until pans are comfortable to touch. ♥Refrigerate, Room, Release, Serve, Store♥

Notes: The top of this one is a little sticky to the touch after baking.

This recipe would not do well in an argument supporting the theory that "all the alcohol bakes out." Brands will make some difference, but three-fourths cup of liqueur might be enough, especially if time to mellow is limited.

Raspberry

This is delicious. It's cool and creamy, smooth and rich in your mouth, yet it leaves a pleasant, comforting, lingering warmth in your chest. It was developed for Gary Thompson in Rochester. He wanted raspberry, but not chocolate. He is Jerry's cousin's husband. See, you never know who will make a simple request that becomes a big hit!

3 pounds cream cheese, room temperature
1 cup granulated sugar
1/3 cup all-purpose flour
4 large eggs, room temperature
1 to 1-1/2 cups (18-ounce jar) raspberry jam or
    preserves (seeds or seedless)*
1 cup heavy cream, room temperature
1 cup crème de cassis or raspberry liqueur
2 teaspoons vanilla

Beat cream cheese in large mixing bowl on low speed about 5 minutes, until smooth and shiny; scrape 2-3 times. Add sugar and beat on low for 2-3 minutes, scraping at least once. Shake flour over batter and beat in. Increase speed one notch and beat 3-4 minutes, scraping several times.

At slow speed again, add eggs one at a time, beating well after each. Scrape after 2nd and 4th eggs, then beat on medium-low for 2 minutes. With mixer back on low, add jam and mix well. Add heavy cream and liqueur slowly and mix for another 3-4 minutes. Add vanilla, beat 2 more minutes. Filling will be a uniform pale raspberry color when thoroughly mixed. Lift beaters and let drip back into bowl.

Pour into 3 prepared 6-inch cheesecake pans. Bake in preheated 400° oven for 15 minutes, then reduce heat to 325° for 1 hour. Turn oven off and cool in closed oven several hours, or until pans are comfortable to touch. ♥Refrigerate, Room, Release, Serve, Store♥

Notes: *It's ok to use up to 1-1/2 cups jam if you don't want any left from 18-ounce jar. Or, use 1 cup in the filling and 1/2 cup for topping.

Presentation ideas: light dollop of raspberry preserves, fresh raspberries artfully arranged, warm raspberry sauce, a really thin drizzle of chocolate. A woven ribbon of thin chocolate glaze and thin raspberry sauce around the top edge is attractive. Or just "I am enough" plain. See Toppings recipes starting on page 114, or use your own.

SECTION VI
Toppings

Any Fruit—Very Easy

1/2 cup preserves
1 tablespoon lemon juice

Mix, heat to gentle boil. Serve warm or cool, drizzled or spread over baked cheesecake.

Any Fruit—Still Easy

1 can (16-1/2 ounces) fruit in light or heavy syrup
    (will be about 1 cup juice <u>and</u> 1 cup fruit)
1 tablespoon cornstarch

Completely drain juice from can and pour into small, heavy saucepan. Add cornstarch and let sit a minute, then stir for a minute. Heat on low medium, stirring occasionally, until mixture begins to thicken, clear and boil. This usually takes 10-15 minutes. Let boil about a minute, then stir fruit in gently and bring back to boil. Serve warm or cool over baked cheese-cake. It's that easy! Stores well in icebox, freezes ok, and can be reheated in microwave.

Notes: If you have a sweet tooth, you may want to add 1 tablespoon of sugar, but try as is first.

Cans of pineapple are just a little bit bigger, but use the same amount of cornstarch. If you use crushed pineapple and add all of it, the sauce will be very thick, more like relish or chutney.

Canned fruit is easy to work with. I especially like Oregon Fruit brand, but use your favorite.

<u>Fresh and frozen</u> are the other two options. The trick with both fresh and frozen fruit is to have enough juice. To use frozen fruit, I pour a one-pound bag of fruit into a large measuring cup, dump <u>1/4 cup of sugar</u> over it, cover the container and let it sit overnight in the icebox. Same works with fresh fruit. You still may not have enough juice, so then you have to add a little water or crush some of the fruit to release juice. Unsweetened fruit requires a little more sugar, but <u>1 tablespoon cornstarch </u>is enough.

Berries have seeds. If you want a gourmet-smooth sauce you'll have to crush, sieve, seed, etc. The point of this book is *Cheesecakes Made Easy*, but most cookbooks and cooking magazines have recipes, often with detailed instructions.

For a slightly different look, puree the fruit and juice in a blender before cooking. This gives a smoother, more sauce-like sauce, so to speak.

Chocolate sauce is easy. Melt chocolate chips or squares with heavy cream or half-and-half for the flavor and consistency you want. Cool cheesecake with hot chocolate sauce is a real treat! Spread a thin layer over the entire cheesecake and allow it to set (may require refrigeration) or drizzle it over individual pieces. These recipes freeze well and reheat conventionally or in microwave. If boiled, they'll thicken, so you'll have to add more cream or half-and-half to thin. Experiment.

Chocolate Sauce

8 ounces (1-1/2 cups) semisweet chocolate chips
1/2 cup heavy cream

Heat and stir in small, heavy pan over very low heat until melted and smooth. DO NOT BOIL. Remove from heat to cool, stirring occasionally, until desired consistency. Drizzle or spread over baked cheese-cake. OR, heat heavy cream in microwave for thirty seconds, then stir in chips until melted and smooth.

Chocolate Satin (Shiny) Glaze

1/4 cup water
1/4 cup sugar
1 cup semisweet chocolate chips

Bring sugar and water to fast boil to dissolve sugar. Remove from heat, add chips, Stir until melted, smooth and desired consistency. Yield: about 2/3 cup.

Coconut-Pecan Topping

1/2 cup heavy cream, room temperature
1/4 cup granulated sugar
1 tablespoon dark brown sugar
1 large egg, room temperature
1-1/2 to 2 teaspoons vanilla (Mexican is good here)
1/4 cup chopped pecans
1/4 cup coconut (I use combo of sweetened and
    unsweetened)
1 teaspoon unsalted butter

Stir all ingredients EXCEPT coconut and pecans
in small saucepan. Cook on medium heat 10-12 minutes,
until thickens and turns yellow-gold-brown. Stir nearly
constantly unless you are using really heavy pan.
Remove from heat and stir in coconut and pecans.
Serve warm or cool, as topping, dollop, or "side dish."
Keeps well in icebox. Yield: 1-1/2 cups

Nut

1/4 cup finely chopped nuts
2 to 4 tablespoons packed brown sugar, dark or light
1 teaspoon cinnamon, if desired

Mix and sprinkle on top of unbaked cheesecake.
For easier chopping, heat nuts in microwave for 2
minutes, or in 325° oven for 5 minutes.

SECTION VII
Miscellaneous Information

Ingredients Tables

The following tables list calorie content (with calories from fat in parentheses), sodium in milligrams (mg) and cholesterol in milligrams. To get an obsessively compulsive count, read labels of the specific ingredients you are using. Brands vary. Salt content varies most; low-fat anything nearly always has more salt. Room is provided to add your ingredients.

A few ingredients are listed, somewhat in order of recipe usage, and in groups of similar items. Not every single ingredient in this book is listed here, nor are they are listed alphabetically. The table to the immediate right is accurate, although not based on the exact recipes given in this book. Brands vary.

Ingredient	Calories (from fat)	Sodium in mg	Cholesterol in mg

Ingredient	Regular	Light
Filling	Calories vary with brand.	
Cream cheese	4,800	3,040
Sugar	720	540
Flour	134	134
Eggs	280	280
Cream	960	960
Half-and-half	280	160
Vanilla	30	40
Subtotal	7,204	5,154
Crust		
Crackers	787	320
Sugar	225	90
Butter	500	400
Subtotal	1,512	810
Total	8,716	5,964
Piece*	484	331

*Three 6-inch cheesecakes cut into 6 slices each = 18

Ingredient	Calories	Sodium	Cholesterol
Cream cheese	(from fat)	in mg	in mg
3 pounds	4,800 (4,320)	4,320	1,440
8 ounces	800 (720)	720	240
1 ounce	100 (90)	90	30
Sugar			
1-1/2 cups	1,080	-0-	-0-
1-1/3 cups	960	-0-	-0-
1-1/4 cups	900	-0-	-0-
1 cup	720	-0-	-0-
2 Tbls	90	-0-	-0-
Flour			
1/3 cup	134	-0-	-0-
Eggs			
One large	70(40)	65	215

Ingredient	Calories	Sodium	Cholesterol
Heavy cream	**(from fat)**	**in mg**	**in mg**
1 cup	960 (800)	80	320
1/2 cup	480 (400)	40	160
Half-and-half			
1 cup	288 (240)	208	80
1/2 cup	144 (120)	104	40
Vanilla			
1 Tbls	30(0)	-0-	-0-
Butter, unsalted	**All fat**		
1 stick (8T)	(800)	-0-	240
5 Tbls	(500)	-0-	150
4 Tbls	(400)	-0-	120

Ingredient	Calories	Sodium	Cholesterol
Keebler Club® Crackers	**(from fat)**	**in mg**	**in mg**
1 package (45)	787 (281)	1,800	-0-
Waverly® Crackers			
1 package (40)	560 (240)	1,280	
Chocolate Morsels			
12 oz pkg	1,610 (805)	-0-	-0-
Unsweet. Chocolate			
8 ounces	1,120 (960)	-0-	-0-

Ingredient	Calories	Sodium	Cholesterol
Jam	**(from fat)**	**in mg**	**in mg**
1-1/2 cups	1,200	240	-0-
1 cup	800	160	-0-
Coconut, Sweet			
1 cup	560 (320)	280	-0-
1/2 cup	280 (160)	140	-0-
Pineapple, Unsweet.			
20-ounce can	315	45	-0-
Nuts, 1 cup			
Macadamia	880 (800)	260	-0-
Walnut	840 (720)	-0-	-0-

Resources

<u>Books I Find Handy</u>

Philadelphia Brand Cream Cheese Cheesecakes
Kraft, Inc.
1989
Publications International, Ltd
7373 North Cicero Avenue
Lincolnwood, IL 60646
ISBN: 0-88176-586-4

The Joy of Cheesecake
Dana Bovbjerg & Jeremy Iggers
1980
Barron's Educational Series, Inc.
250 Wireless Boulevard
Hauppauge, New York 11788
ISBN: 0-8120-5350-8

The Recipe Writer's Handbook
Barbara Gibbs Ostmann & Jane L. Baker
1997
John Wiley & Sons, Inc.
605 Third Avenue
New York, NY 10158-0012
ISBN: 0-471-17294-4

Ingredients

Tadco/Niblack
900 Jefferson Rd, Bldg 6
Rochester, NY 14623
1-800-724-8883
Ingredientwarehouse.com

They have it all!
Doug & Nancy are
always helpful.

Site in progress

Dot.coms for utensils, ingredients, information, fun, recipes, etc. I've ordered from several. Some of these are pretty fancy sites. It's a great way to find out which companies own your favorite foods.

Acemart.com
Bakery-net.com
Baking.m-ms.com
Bestfoods.com
Bettycrocker.com
Cakedeco.com
Chefscatalog.com
Dole-plantation.com
Dominosugar.com
Enterprisebox.com
Fantes.com
Happycookers.com

Hersheys.com
Imperialholly.com
KitchenAid.com
Oregonfruit.com
Ravensbergen.com
Verybestbaking.com

Feel free to contact the author with any questions, comments or concerns. Please reference "CME" in subject line and email to: marcymallory@earthlink.net

About the Author

Originally this book was a collection of recipes gathered over twenty years. Food is so entwined in who we are; recipe drawers reflect patterns and changes in our lives. Haute cuisine, vegetarian, low-fat, raw, no-sugar, soup and salad, juices, protein—phases we all go through. However, copyright issues were major. I give myself permission.

Since I always want to know about authors, here's my info. I was born in the panhandle of Texas on the same day and year Prince Charles was born. Go figure. I have no children, started college when I was sixteen, wandered through life and completed my B.S. degree in Rehabilitation Science at thirty-two, continued on for a master's degree (Human Development) and really never "used" either of them.

Currently, I am a massage therapist. My fascination with energy work and my obsession with Oriental medicine are infused into my work, and into me. I love to learn, and will be taking classes on the way to my funeral; hopefully, I'll have learned how to exit this world with grace. I believe it's good to be kind and gentle, but struggle with the concept that I have to take care of myself first. Reading, baking, gardening and listening to music are my favorite things. More and more, I believe in synchronicity, but I struggle with lack of patience. Now!

A video to accompany this book is underway. A collection of short stories about women's real fantasies has been bouncing around for ten years. A new-age novel has been swirling and gaining momentum for about a year. I also want to check out modeling for "mature women" because I've always frozen in front of cameras and hated pictures of myself. I may not be quite tall enough. Another goal is to be on the David Letterman show. They ignored me several years ago when I emailed them about my idea to have a shared-birthday show with a regular person (that would be me, myself and I) and a world-famous person like Prince Charles. I wish I were courageous enough to travel the world during disasters, helping however I could, but that will remain a fantasy. Lastly, I'm going to live to one hundred twenty years old in great physical, mental, emotional and spiritual health.

That's me in a nutshell. I hope you've enjoyed the book. Thanks for the opportunity to share an item from my "someday I'm going to" list. Good luck!

Marcy

Order
Page
on
Other
Side

CHEESECAKES MADE EASY

Please contact the author directly for
quantity discount prices. Please reference
"CME" in subject line.

Email: marcymallory@earthlink.net

128

Order Form: Send _____ copies of *Cheesecakes Made Easy* to:

Name: _____

Address: _____

City _____State _____Zip: _____

Telephone: _____

Email address: _____

I understand that I may return any item for a full refund.

Shipping: U.S. $3.50 for first book and $2.00 for each additional.

Sales tax: Please add 7.75% for items shipped to Texas addresses.

Texas: 1 book: $14.95 +1.15 = $16.10 + 3.50 = $19.60 _____
Texas: 2 books: $29.90 +2.30 = $32.20 + 5.50 = $37.70 _____

Other: 1 book: $14.95 + 3.50 = $18.45 _____
Other: 2 books: $29.90 + 5.50 = $ 35.40 _____

Total amount of order: $_____

Payment: Check Credit Card

Visa ___ MasterCard ____ AMEX _____

Card number: _____

Name on card: _____ Exp. Date: _____/_____

Postal orders: CME by Marcy Mallory
PO Box 201224, Arlington, Texas 76011

Email orders: marcymallory@earthlink.net.
Please reference "CME" in subject line.